Hey! I Can Read This!

Hey! I Can Read This!

The Interactive Book Experience

By

Donna Sabino Butt &

Kathy Barlow Thurman

Crystal Springs
BOOKS

A Division of Staff Development for Educators (SDE)

Peterborough, New Hampshire

Published by Crystal Springs Books
75 Jaffrey Road
P.O. Box 500
Peterborough, NH 03458
1-800-321-0401
www.sde.com; www.crystalsprings.com

Publisher Cataloging-in-Publication Data (U.S.)

Butt, Donna Sabino.
    Hey! I can read this! : the interactive book experience / Donna Sabino Butt,
& Kathy Barlow Thurman . —1st ed.
[128] p. : ill. , photos ;   cm.
Includes index.
Includes reproducibles, instructions, and verses for 29 interactive books
covering language, math, science, geography and other skills.
ISBN 1-884548-38-5
1. Teaching – Aids and devices.   2. Elementary school teaching.
I. Thurman, Kathy Barlow. II. Title.
372.13 21   CIP   LB1555.B88 2001
2001 135929

Editor: Sandra J. Taylor
Art Director and Photographer: Soosen Dunholter
Illustrator: Patrick Belfiori

DEDICATION

To my parents, Claude ("Bugs") and Pat Barlow.
I will always love you, "...all the way up to the sky."
KBT

To my parents, Vic and Lil Sabino. I recall with a smile all those little things you have done for me—and
the not so little, too. You have taught me more than any book ever could.
There will never be a day when I won't smile a quiet smile and say an unspoken thanks.
I love you!

DSB

Acknowledgments

Thanks to:

My sons, Jason and Josh Sankovitch, for your love. Without you, my heart would be smaller, my life duller.

My husband, Jeff Thurman, for your love of life and your belief in me.

My brother, Bruce, and my sister, Wendy, for our shared childhood experiences.

My grandmother, Luretha Wynn Cross, for showing me how to age with grace.

My grandmother, Mae Barlow Tucker, for encouraging me to become a teacher.

My editor, Sandy Taylor, for the patience and kind guidance you used to help us bring this book into existence.

My book-writing partner and best friend, Donna, for helping to preserve my sanity through laughter.

Hey, Donna, we did it!

KBT

Thanks to:

Greg, who is so essential in my life. Thank you for all your support, input, and understanding over the years. You make a difference in every day. You have provided me with a spoonful of stars to wish upon. I love you more!

Terri, Cheri, Vic, Nick, and Shelia, who have helped me find a special outlook on life. Thanks for all the good times and the bad. But most of all, the memories that we share will add so much to my tomorrows.

All the "little people" who have inspired me. Jake, Nicklas, Gabriella, J.T., Jesse, Ivanna, and Creighton, thanks for adding your own unique aspects that light my path in life.

Jim and Shirley Butt. I have noticed all the thoughtful little things you do for me. Thank you for the encouragement.

Kathy. Please take a moment and realize the overwhelming impact our friendship has made. Dreams do come true! Thanks for adding a little humor to my life! I love ya!

DSB

TABLE OF CONTENTS

Continued

INTRODUCTION

DEAR TEACHERS,

Our school day is filled with the challenge to promote learning in young children using various language activities. We do so with the goals of teaching reading and language enrichment in mind. But have you ever longed for something *new* and *exciting* to use with your students? Or wondered what you could add to your curriculum that would captivate and inspire your students and increase their success? As classroom teachers, we certainly have, which is part of the reason we developed our interactive books.

One thing we noticed in our own classrooms was that our Book Centers were not exactly the most popular places, despite displays of wonderful literature, comfortable bean bags and cushions, and reading props used to entice our students. We wanted them to be more involved with books and found that the ones that really captured their attention and held their interest were those that they could manipulate or interact with, such as *How Many Bugs in a Box?* by David Carter and *The Very Hungry Caterpillar* by Eric Carle.

As we brainstormed to find a solution to this issue, we created our first two-dimensional interactive book, knowing that the children loved to sing, work puzzles, and use books with which they could interact. We put ours to the test by first introducing it to the children as a group, teaching them how to sing the song and manipulate the pages. With our fingers crossed, we watched the children actively engaged in our book. Success! Their excitement was contagious and soon we were creating more of these. Over the years, we've kept the hits, reevaluated the misses, and grown our library to more than 25 interactive books.

Teachers, we wholeheartedly encourage you to make these books. You will have a wonderful time with your children, singing the words and manipulating the pieces. In addition, you can give yourselves a pat on the back for opening a whole new world of learning experiences to your young students.

HAPPY INTERACTING,

Kathy and Donna

WHAT ARE INTERACTIVE BOOKS AND WHY USE THEM?

Interactive books have parts or pieces that children can manipulate while reading the text. In our books these pieces are attached to Velcro and can be moved from one part of the book to another. Our text consists of verses that have been set to familiar tunes so the children can interact both musically (sing the text) and through fine motor movement (manipulating the book pieces).

Although we basically stumbled upon creating interactive books and were thrilled with the success the children experienced with them, we later found research that supported their use and gave a rationale as to why they really work…and they truly do!

Studies show that to build brainpower:
- Use music as a powerful way to present information and aid retention.
- Make use of repetitive text and language patterns.
- Practice skills that provide immediate feedback.
- Use the fingers to stimulate the brain and develop fine motor skills.
- Add novelty to instruction to boost memory.
- Use confidence builders (and confidence is best built by repetition).
- Engage cross-modalities (i.e., visual and auditory).
- Revisit information often to enhance memory.
- Engage, involve, and stimulate the emotions.

Our interactive books achieve all of the above! In addition, they are beneficial to teachers as well as students for the following reasons:

- They are original, fresh, and exciting for everyone!

- They are relatively inexpensive to make and are highly durable; they last for years.

- They can be made by teachers, aides, parents, volunteers, and students as young as fourth and fifth graders with adult guidance.

- The books are loved by children and fun to use by those of all ability levels.

- The books range from simple to more challenging. For example, *Mr. Square*, a basic book, would be used at the start of the school year, whereas *Oceans* would be introduced later in the year.

- The books are skill- and theme-oriented, and have language extension activities.

- Children no longer have to wait for the teacher to have time to read to them. Once these books have been demonstrated to the children a few times, pre-readers and readers alike can use them independently while the teacher is busy instructing a small group.

- Singing the words to a familiar tune enables the students to retain the text and helps them memorize it, which is an important step in learning to read.

- The children read and sing the books over and over again (once is never enough!) and gain a real sense of accomplishment when they complete them.

- The books have versatile uses and may be implemented in a large or small group, by two or three students, or independently.

- Since two or three children usually choose to do a book together, they have opportunities for peer tutoring, turn taking, sharing, social interaction, and language enrichment.

- An interactive book is a center in and of itself! It can be used anywhere in the classroom (except the water table, for obvious reasons). We put our books in baskets and on shelves and rotate them every week or two, just as we do center activities.

How to Make Interactive Books

You don't need to be a gifted artist or musician to make and use interactive books; we're not. For the artwork in our books, we used patterns, cookie cutters, clip art, coloring books, stickers, and stamps. We also begged artistic colleagues for help (and bribed them with the promise of sharing the book with them once it was complete!). As for singing, as long as we're loud, enthusiastic, and cheerful, the children don't seem to notice when we're off-key.

Naturally, our books are more quickly and easily made once you have the patterns, text, and tunes supplied, as you do here. Then it's simply a matter of copying, coloring, cutting, and pasting for you, your aide, or parent volunteers. We also ask fourth- and fifth-grade teachers at our school to make the books for us as a classroom project. It's an ideal way for the students to learn how to follow directions. They enjoy creating the books and coming back at later times to have our children sing and read the books to them.

Still, at first glance, you may feel that these would require more time than you have. Don't panic! This isn't brain surgery. In the pages that follow, we give generic instructions for making our books. Then, with each individual project, we point out any specific steps that might vary from book to book, such as the arrangement of the art, the size of the book, or the placement of the binding. Once you've made one book, the others will be self-explanatory as they all follow the same basic procedures. We've taken creative license with each one of our books and you should feel free to do the same.

Basic Materials List

- Poster board, tagboard, or construction paper (reinforce the latter by gluing it to a stiffer material)—for the book's backboard and pages. In most cases 12" x 18" works well for the backboard and 4 ½" x 12" for the book pages.
- Plain white paper and/or construction paper—for permanent artwork and the manipulatives
- Water-based colored markers (permanent markers bleed through materials)
- Crayons
- Scissors
- Rubber cement or glue sticks
- Ruler
- Velcro (self-stick)
- Laminating film and machine
- Book-binding material, or rings of choice

Instructions

1. Cut the backboard and book pages from the material of choice.

2. Photocopy the text to the size desired for the title/tune page, book pages, and sometimes the backboard.

3. Color the reproducibles with crayons or water-based markers, or copy onto construction paper of different colors.

4. Make sure the artwork on the backboard is placed high enough above the bottom edge so that it will not be obscured when the book pages are in an upward position.

5. Use regular or shape scissors for cutting out the text.

6. Affix the text and permanent pieces of art to the book pages and/or backboard with glue or rubber cement.

7. Laminate everything at least once, sometimes twice.

8. After everything has been laminated, attach one part of a piece of Velcro to the back of each manipulative and the other part of the Velcro to an appropriate place on the book pages and/or the backboard.

9. Arrange the book pages in order, stack and align them with the backboard, then bind the book across the bottom—or on the left side, depending on the style of your book. Or punch holes in the pages and backboard and bind with rings or other materials of your choice. (See Helpful Hints, page 18, for additional information.)

 HEY! I CAN READ THIS!

SAMPLE PAGES
FOR INTERACTIVE BOOK PROJECTS

Skill(s) included for each book

Special instructions for individual books

Title/tune book page

Book page with verse, artwork, and/or manipulative

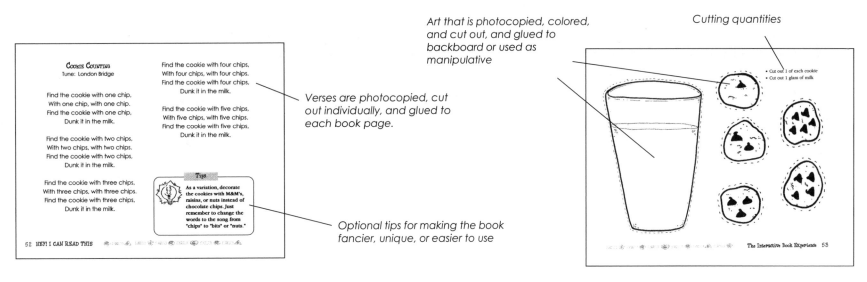

Placement for manipulative on book page

Backboard

Art that is photocopied, colored, and cut out, and glued to backboard or used as manipulative

Cutting quantities

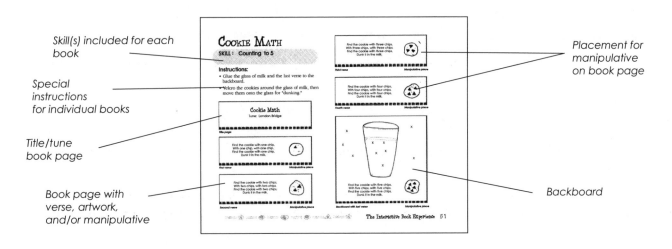

Verses are photocopied, cut out individually, and glued to each book page.

Optional tips for making the book fancier, unique, or easier to use

         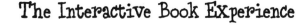

HELPFUL HINTS

1. For a decorative border, use shape scissors to cut out the book's text.

2. Instead of coloring the patterns with markers, try photocopying them on construction paper.

3. To make the manipulative pieces stronger, run them through the laminator twice.

4. If the lamination doesn't seal well, put the laminated pieces between two sheets of paper and iron over them, using dry heat.

5. BE CREATIVE! Use foil paper, cupcake liners, wiggly eyes, doilies, wallpaper, stickers, ink stamps, colored tape, gift wrap, fabric, window stickers, glitter; the list is unlimited.

6. If a binding machine isn't available, use book rings, chicken rings, pipe cleaners, yarn, ribbon, or other materials of choice.

7. Add a "belt" to each book to hold the pages together when it's not in use. To make a belt, use poster board or tagboard and cut a strip 1" wide and 3" longer than the width of your book. Attach the belt to the book with Velcro.

Please Note: In this book, we've included reproducibles that can be used for the artwork. If you prefer, however, to individualize your books, feel free to create your own illustrations and use them instead.

How to Introduce and Use Interactive Books

THE TEACHER:

1. Introduce an interactive book during a large group session and choose one that relates to that week's theme/skills.
2. Model using the book by holding it up so all can see it and singing the text while manipulating the pieces. Help the children learn to have their fingers close to, or actually touching, the Velcro when they manipulate the pieces.
3. Remind the children that when they use the book to be sure to lay it flat on the floor or a table. Demonstrate.
4. Sing and manipulate the book several times in a row so the children become very familiar with it. They'll remind you with, "Read it again!"
5. Put the book out in centers.

THE CHILD:

1. The child lays the book flat on the floor or on a table.
2. The child who is going to read the book opens it to the first page, sings the verse printed there, and moves the manipulative piece to the appropriate place on the backboard page. The reader follows this procedure through to the book's end.
3. Often, two or three children will read and sing a book together. We encourage this as it fosters social relationship skills, such as sharing and cooperating, and it allows for peer tutoring.
4. To complete the interactive book, the child removes the manipulative pieces from the backboard and returns them to their original places by matching them to the identical pieces glued to that page. This reinforces task completion.

How Interactive Books Fit into the Curriculum

A great advantage to interactive books is that once they've been modeled to the children, they can be put out in the classroom and used entirely independently by the children. An interactive book is a center in and of itself! Following are ways to expand the uses of these books.

Language Extension Activities

- **Mystery Box Words**
  Write selected words from the book, one per card, and put the cards in a mystery box (or a sack, if you don't have a box). Children draw out one card at a time and search the book until they find the word.

- **Word Card Game**
  Write words (one per card) from the books on cards. Stack the cards and place them face down. Children take turns turning a card over and finding the word in the book.

- **Post-it Note Word Match**
  Write words on Post-it notes and have the children find those words in the book and attach the note to them.

- **Block Sentences**
  Attach cards with the text (one word per card) to wooden blocks in the block center. Children arrange the blocks in order to sequence the sentence.

- **Sentences in a Basket**
  Write one sentence per strip of paper and put them in a basket. Let the children pull out a strip and find that sentence in the book.

- **Spell It**
  Let the children use avalanche letters or magnetic letters and a magnetic board to reproduce the text.

- **Vowels**

  Provide highlighting tape and let the children cover each vowel they locate in one of the verses, or assign each child a different verse and have them compare results as a peer tutoring/checking activity.

- **Extend the Story**

  Offer children paper, pencil, and crayons and suggest they extend the story by drawing and writing about what could happen next.

- **Write a Character**

  Provide paper, pencil, and an envelope and let the children write a letter to the character in the book. Once they've done that, it's your turn to write them back (in the role of that character, of course!).

- **Letter Stamps**

  Provide ink pads and alphabet letter stamps and have the children reproduce the text by stamping it on paper.

- **Child Illustrators**

  Give the children the text on paper, leaving about half of the page blank. Let the children illustrate the text in a new and original way.

- **Graphic Organizers**

  After reading the book, use a graphic organizer such as a word web to organize information from the text.

- **Daily News**

  Have the children use as many words as possible from the book when writing the Daily News. Underline those words.

- **Word Chains**

  Provide strips of construction paper and let the children print words from a sentence in the text on them, one word per strip. Children then connect the words in the correct order to make a sentence paper chain.

- **Hands Up**

  Have the children raise both hands up into the air when they read or hear rhyming words in the text.

- **Syllables**

  Have the children find one-, two-, and three-syllable words in each book and clap the syllables.

- **Word Challenge**

  Have a child write a word from the text on a Write On, Wipe Off board and challenge another child to say the word or find it in the text.

Are We There Yet?

SKILL: Geography

Instructions:

- Color each individual state a different color but use the same color for the same state in the grouped states.

- Glue the last verse and the grouped states to the backboard.

- Mark an "X" on the grouped states shape to help children learn the correct location of each individual state.

Are We There Yet?

Tune: Darlin' Clementine

Title page

Are we there yet?
Are we there yet?
Are we there, in Florida?
We are driving through Kentucky,
Maybe the next state is Florida.

First verse   *Manipulative piece*

Are we there yet?
Are we there yet?
Are we there, in Florida?
We are driving through Tennessee,
Maybe the next state is Florida.

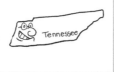

Second verse   *Manipulative piece*

Are we there yet?
Are we there yet?
Are we there, in Florida?
We are driving through Alabama,
Maybe the next state is Florida.

Third verse   *Manipulative piece*

Are we there yet?
Are we there yet?
Are we there, in Florida?
We are driving through Georgia,
Maybe the next state is Florida.

Fourth verse   *Manipulative piece*

We are here now!
We are here now!
We are here, in Florida.
I really have to use the bathroom,
Now that we're here, in Florida!

Backboard with last verse   *Manipulative piece*

ARE WE THERE YET?

Tune: Darlin' Clementine

Are we there yet?
Are we there yet?
Are we there, in Florida?
We are driving through Kentucky,
Maybe the next state is Florida.

Are we there yet?
Are we there yet?
Are we there, in Florida?
We are driving through Tennessee,
Maybe the next state is Florida.

Are we there yet?
Are we there yet?
Are we there, in Florida?
We are driving through Alabama,
Maybe the next state is Florida.

Are we there yet?
Are we there yet?
Are we there, in Florida?
We are driving through Georgia,
Maybe the next state is Florida.

We are here now!
We are here now!
We are here, in Florida.
I really have to use the bathroom,
Now that we're here, in Florida!

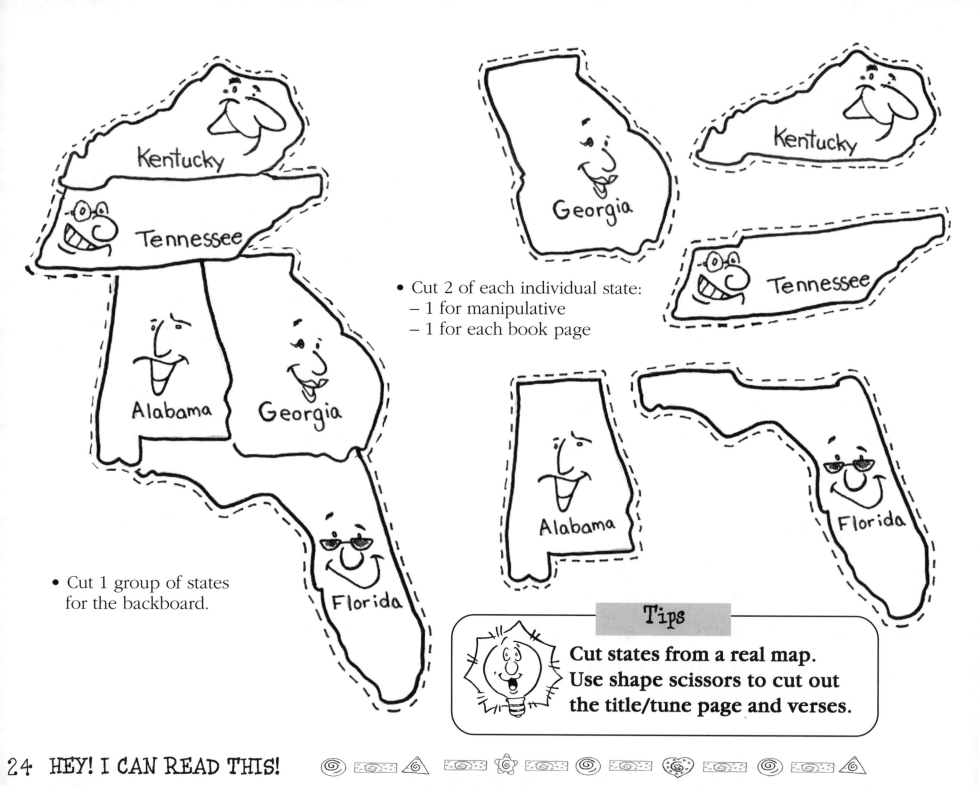

- Cut 2 of each individual state:
  - 1 for manipulative
  - 1 for each book page

- Cut 1 group of states for the backboard.

Tips

Cut states from a real map.
Use shape scissors to cut out
the title/tune page and verses.

BIRTHDAY ADDITION

SKILL: Addition

Instructions:

- Glue the cake and plate and the last verse to the backboard.

- Glue 1 candle to the top of the cake.

Birthday Addition

Tune: Farmer in the Dell

Title page

1 plus 1 makes 2,
1 plus 1 makes 2,
Hi, ho, it's adding you know,
1 plus 1 makes 2.

First verse   *Manipulative piece*

2 plus 1 makes 3,
2 plus 1 makes 3,
Hi, ho, it's adding you know,
2 plus 1 makes 3.

Second verse   *Manipulative piece*

3 plus 1 makes 4,
3 plus 1 makes 4,
Hi, ho, it's adding you know,
3 plus 1 makes 4.

Third verse   *Manipulative piece*

4 plus 1 makes 5,
4 plus 1 makes 5,
Hi, ho, it's adding you know,
4 plus 1 makes 5.

Backboard with last verse   *Manipulative piece*

Birthday Addition

Tune: Farmer in the Dell

1 plus 1 makes 2,
1 plus 1 makes 2,
Hi, ho, it's adding you know,
1 plus 1 makes 2.

3 plus 1 makes 4,
3 plus 1 makes 4,
Hi, ho, it's adding you know,
3 plus 1 makes 4.

2 plus 1 makes 3,
2 plus 1 makes 3,
Hi, ho, it's adding you know,
2 plus 1 makes 3.

4 plus 1 makes 5,
4 plus 1 makes 5,
Hi, ho, it's adding you know,
4 plus 1 makes 5.

Tip

Use glitter to add sparkle to the flames and/or to decorate the cake.

- Cut 9 candles:
  - 4 for manipulatives
  - 1 for cake
  - 4 for book pages

- Cut 1 cake on a plate for the backboard.
- Glue 1 candle to the top of the cake.

CHICKEN POX

Instructions:

- Glue the last verse to the backboard.
- Number each chicken pox and piece of Velcro to encourage numeral matching and recognition.
- If desired, draw and color additional spots on the title page.
- Begin the book by moving the chicken pox from the pages onto the boy's face. Then reverse the procedure.

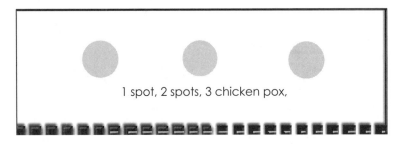

Title page

1 spot, 2 spots, 3 chicken pox,

First verse · **3 Manipulative pieces**

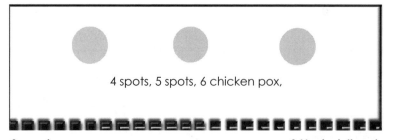

4 spots, 5 spots, 6 chicken pox,

Second verse · **3 Manipulative pieces**

7 spots, 8 spots, 9 chicken pox,

Third verse · **3 Manipulative pieces**

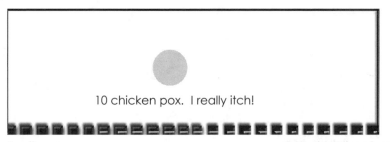

10 chicken pox. I really itch!

Fourth verse · **1 Manipulative piece**

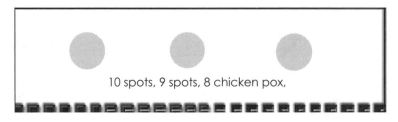

10 spots, 9 spots, 8 chicken pox,

Fifth verse · **3 Manipulative pieces**

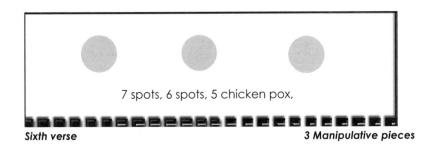

7 spots, 6 spots, 5 chicken pox,

Sixth verse　　　　　　　　　　　**3 Manipulative pieces**

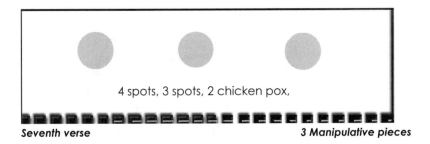

4 spots, 3 spots, 2 chicken pox,

Seventh verse　　　　　　　　　　　**3 Manipulative pieces**

1 chicken pox and now I'm well!

Backboard with last verse　　　　　　**1 Manipulative piece**

CHICKEN POX

Tune: Ten Little Indians

1 spot, 2 spots, 3 chicken pox,

4 spots, 5 spots, 6 chicken pox,

7 spots, 8 spots, 9 chicken pox,

10 chicken pox. I really itch!

10 spots, 9 spots, 8 chicken pox,

7 spots, 6 spots, 5 chicken pox,

4 spots, 3 spots, 2 chicken pox,

1 chicken pox and now I'm well!

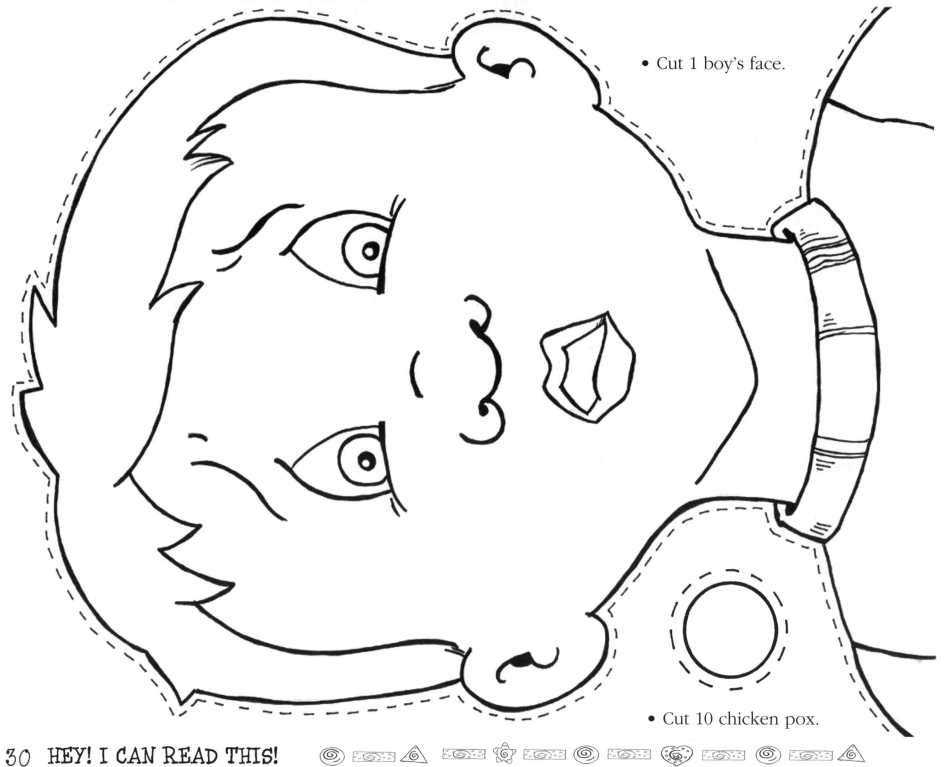

• Cut 1 boy's face.

• Cut 10 chicken pox.

30 HEY! I CAN READ THIS!

CHOCOLATE CANDY

SKILLS: Shapes and shape words

Instructions:

- When you use this book, the pieces of candy should be on the backboard (in the box of candy). Then, as the reading/singing begins, they are moved out of the box and onto the individual pages.

Chocolate Candy

Tune: Happy Birthday

Title page

Have a piece of my candy,
Have a piece of my candy,
Take a chocolate **circle**,
Have a piece of my candy.

First verse — *Manipulative piece*

Have a piece of my candy,
Have a piece of my candy,
Take a chocolate **square**,
Have a piece of my candy.

Second verse — *Manipulative piece*

Have a piece of my candy,
Have a piece of my candy,
Take a chocolate **triangle**,
Have a piece of my candy.

Third verse — *Manipulative piece*

Have a piece of my candy,
Have a piece of my candy,
Take a chocolate **rectangle**,
Have a piece of my candy.

Fourth verse — *Manipulative piece*

Have a piece of my candy,
Have a piece of my candy,
Take a chocolate **star**,
Have a piece of my candy.

Fifth verse — *Manipulative piece*

Have a piece of my candy,
Have a piece of my candy,
Take a chocolate **oval**,
Have a piece of my candy.

Sixth verse — *Manipulative piece*

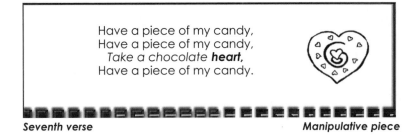

Have a piece of my candy,
Have a piece of my candy,
*Take a chocolate **heart**,*
Have a piece of my candy.

Seventh verse　　　　　　　　　*Manipulative piece*

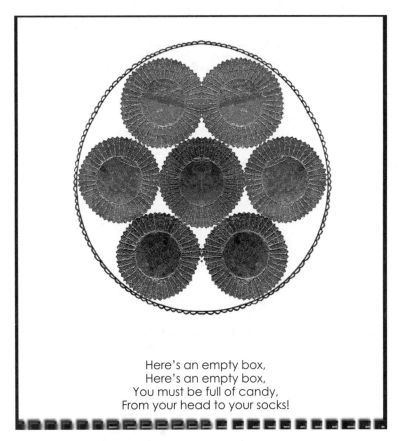

Here's an empty box,
Here's an empty box,
You must be full of candy,
From your head to your socks!

Backboard with last verse

CHOCOLATE CANDY

Tune: Happy Birthday

Have a piece of my candy,
Have a piece of my candy,
Take a chocolate circle,
Have a piece of my candy.

Have a piece of my candy,
Have a piece of my candy,
Take a chocolate square,
Have a piece of my candy.

Have a piece of my candy,
Have a piece of my candy,
Take a chocolate triangle,
Have a piece of my candy.

Have a piece of my candy,
Have a piece of my candy,
Take a chocolate rectangle,
Have a piece of my candy.

Have a piece of my candy,
Have a piece of my candy,
Take a chocolate star,
Have a piece of my candy.

Have a piece of my candy,
Have a piece of my candy,
Take a chocolate oval,
Have a piece of my candy.

Have a piece of my candy,
Have a piece of my candy,
Take a chocolate heart,
Have a piece of my candy.

Here's an empty box,
Here's an empty box,
You must be full of candy,
From your head to your socks!

Tip

Use foil cupcake liners as candy cups.

Cut 2 of each piece of candy:
- –1 for manipulative
- –1 for each book page

 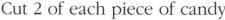

CLOUDS

Instructions:

- Glue the cloud shapes and the verse to the backboard. Be sure to place the verse high enough so the book pages don't cover any part of it.

- Repeat and sing the same verse for each page of manipulatives.

- Instead of cutting the book pages, tear the top edge to resemble clouds.

Clouds
Tune: Turkey in the Straw

Title page

A car

First page   **Manipulative piece**

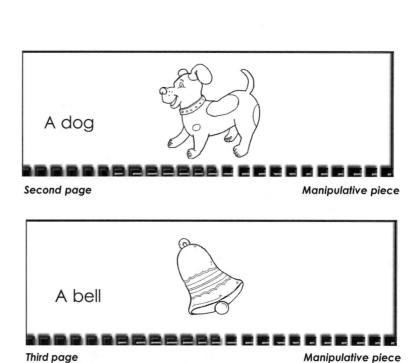

A dog

Second page   **Manipulative piece**

A bell

Third page   **Manipulative piece**

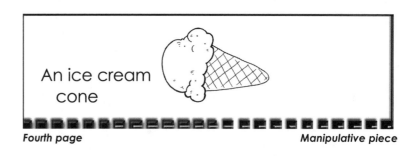

An ice cream cone

Fourth page   **Manipulative piece**

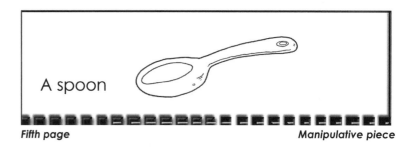

A spoon

Fifth page   **Manipulative piece**

What's in the blue sky?
High, high, high.
What's in the blue sky?
High, high, high.
What's in the blue sky?
High, high, high.
What's in the sky, my darling?

Clouds
Tune: Turkey in the Straw

Backboard with verse

CLOUDS

Tune: Turkey in the Straw

What's in the blue sky?

High, high, high.

What's in the blue sky?

High, high, high.

What's in the blue sky?

High, high, high.

What's in the sky, my darling?

Tip

To create other cloud shapes look in clip-art books for pictures.

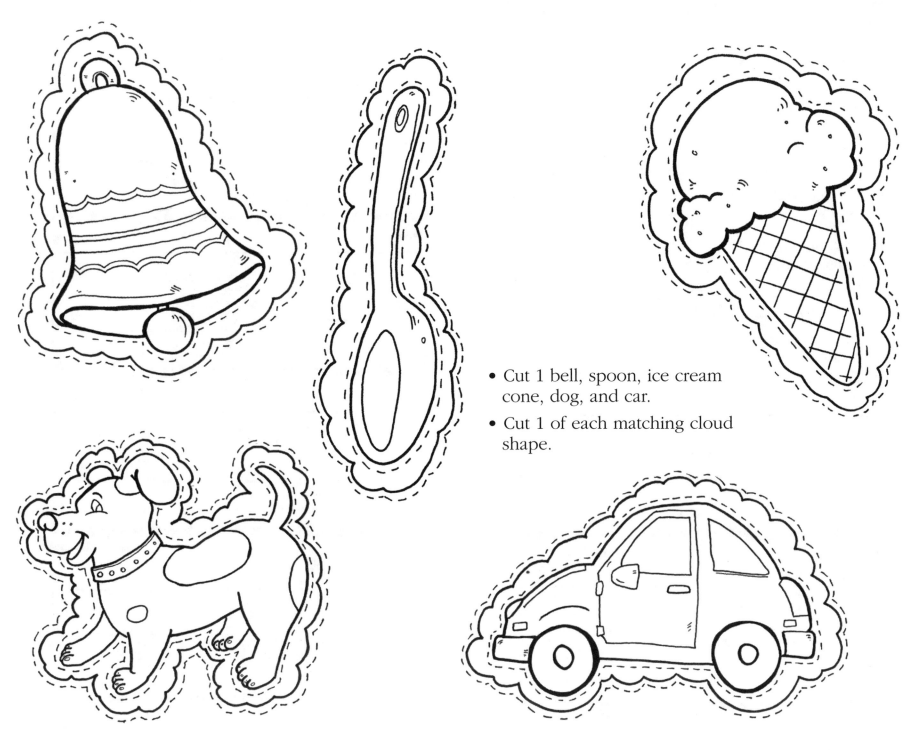

- Cut 1 bell, spoon, ice cream cone, dog, and car.
- Cut 1 of each matching cloud shape.

COLOR FISH

Instructions:

- Cut out the backboard in the shape of a fishbowl.

- Cut water out of blue construction paper and glue to the backboard.

- Write, highlight, or underline color words with colored markers.

- The last verse of the book is on a separate book page—not glued to the backboard.

- Arrange the rocks around the bottom of the fishbowl.

Color Fish
Tune: Where is Thumbkin?

Title page

Where is **orange** fish?
Where is **orange** fish?
Here I am. Here I am.
Hiding in the fishbowl.
Hiding in the fishbowl.
Blub, blub, blub,
Blub, blub, blub.

First verse   **Manipulative piece**

Where is **red** fish?
Where is **red** fish?
Here I am. Here I am.
Hiding in the fishbowl.
Hiding in the fishbowl.
Blub, blub, blub,
Blub, blub, blub.

Second verse   **Manipulative piece**

Where is **blue** fish?
Where is **blue** fish?
Here I am. Here I am.
Hiding in the fishbowl.
Hiding in the fishbowl.
Blub, blub, blub,
Blub, blub, blub.

Third verse   **Manipulative piece**

Where is **pink** fish?
Where is **pink** fish?
Here I am. Here I am.
Hiding in the fishbowl.
Hiding in the fishbowl.
Blub, blub, blub,
Blub, blub, blub.

Fourth verse   **Manipulative piece**

Where is **black** fish?
Where is **black** fish?
Here I am. Here I am.
Hiding in the fishbowl.
Hiding in the fishbowl.
Blub, blub, blub,
Blub, blub, blub.

Fifth verse   **Manipulative piece**

Where is **yellow** fish?
Where is **yellow** fish?
Here I am. Here I am.
Hiding in the fishbowl.
Hiding in the fishbowl.
Blub, blub, blub,
Blub, blub, blub.

Sixth verse   *Manipulative piece*

Where is **brown** fish?
Where is **brown** fish?
Here I am. Here I am.
Hiding in the fishbowl.
Hiding in the fishbowl.
Blub, blub, blub,
Blub, blub, blub.

Seventh verse   *Manipulative piece*

Where is **white** fish?
Where is **white** fish?
Here I am. Here I am.
Hiding in the fishbowl.
Hiding in the fishbowl.
Blub, blub, blub,
Blub, blub, blub.

Eighth verse   *Manipulative piece*

Where is **green** fish?
Where is **green** fish?
Here I am. Here I am.
Hiding in the fishbowl.
Hiding in the fishbowl.
Blub, blub, blub,
Blub, blub, blub.

Ninth verse   *Manipulative piece*

Where is **purple** fish?
Where is **purple** fish?
Here I am. Here I am.
Hiding in the fishbowl.
Hiding in the fishbowl.
Blub, blub, blub,
Blub, blub, blub.

Last verse   *Manipulative piece*

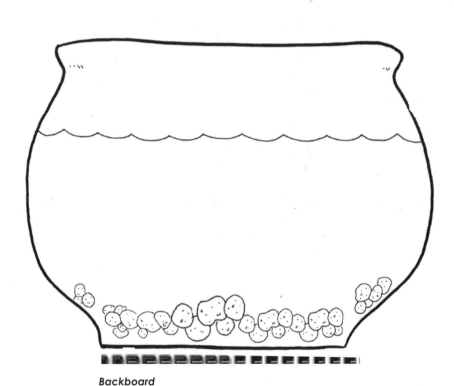

Backboard

Color Fish

Tune: Where is Thumbkin?

Where is **orange** fish?
Where is **orange** fish?
Here I am. Here I am.
Hiding in the fishbowl.
Hiding in the fishbowl.
Blub, blub, blub,
Blub, blub, blub.

Where is **red** fish?
Where is **red** fish?
Here I am. Here I am.
Hiding in the fishbowl.
Hiding in the fishbowl.
Blub, blub, blub,
Blub, blub, blub.

Where is **blue** fish?
Where is **blue** fish?
Here I am. Here I am.
Hiding in the fishbowl.
Hiding in the fishbowl.
Blub, blub, blub,
Blub, blub, blub.

Where is **pink** fish?
Where is **pink** fish?
Here I am. Here I am.
Hiding in the fishbowl.
Hiding in the fishbowl.
Blub, blub, blub,
Blub, blub, blub.

Where is **black** fish?
Where is **black** fish?
Here I am. Here I am.
Hiding in the fishbowl.
Hiding in the fishbowl.
Blub, blub, blub,
Blub, blub, blub.

Where is **yellow** fish?
Where is **yellow** fish?
Here I am. Here I am.
Hiding in the fishbowl.
Hiding in the fishbowl.
   Blub, blub, blub,
   Blub, blub, blub.

Where is **brown** fish?
Where is **brown** fish?
Here I am. Here I am.
Hiding in the fishbowl.
Hiding in the fishbowl.
   Blub, blub, blub,
   Blub, blub, blub.

Where is **white** fish?
Where is **white** fish?
Here I am. Here I am.
Hiding in the fishbowl.
Hiding in the fishbowl.
   Blub, blub, blub,
   Blub, blub, blub.

Where is **green** fish?
Where is **green** fish?
Here I am. Here I am.
Hiding in the fishbowl.
Hiding in the fishbowl.
   Blub, blub, blub,
   Blub, blub, blub.

Where is **purple** fish?
Where is **purple** fish?
Here I am. Here I am.
Hiding in the fishbowl.
Hiding in the fishbowl.
   Blub, blub, blub,
   Blub, blub, blub.

- Cut out fish and color each one a different color: orange, red, blue, pink, black, yellow, brown, white, green, and purple. Use markers or cut from colored construction paper.

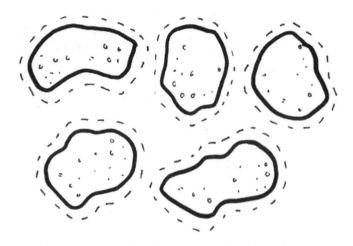

- Cut out several rock shapes and glue them around the bottom of the fishbowl, overlapping them in places.

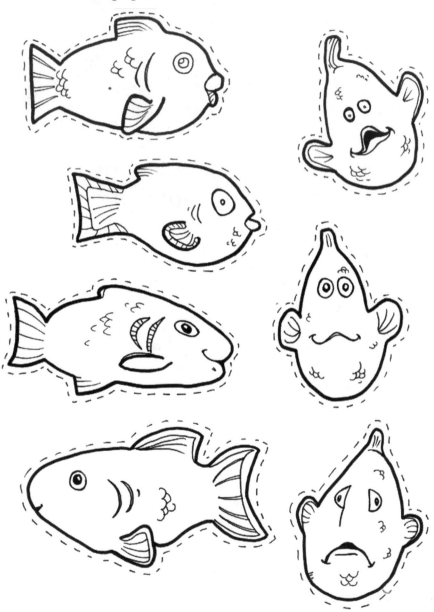

• Enlarge the fishbowl pattern to the desired size and cut 1.

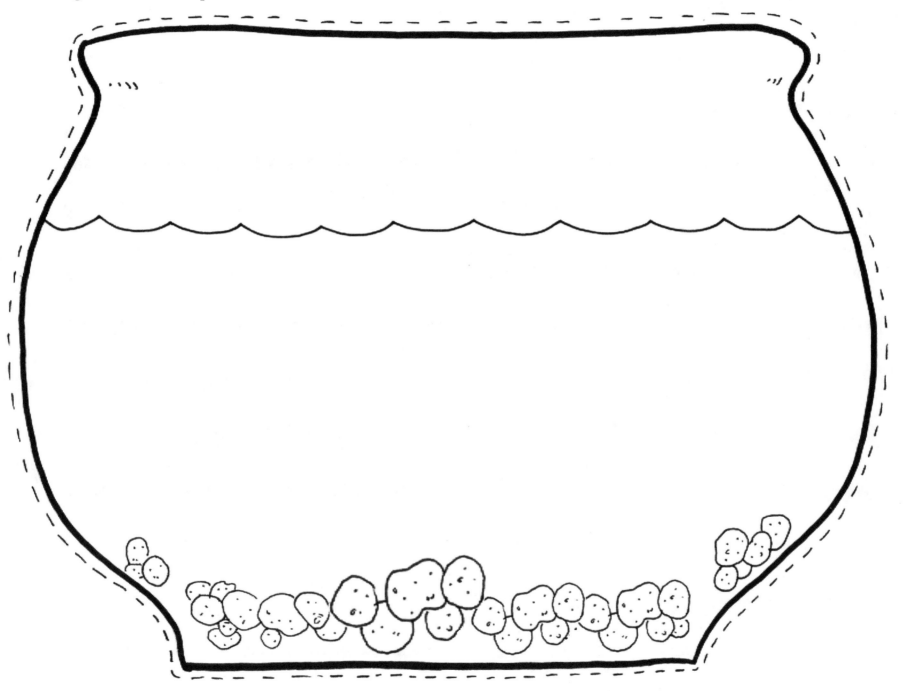

CONTINENTS

Instructions:

- The continents may be any color you wish—just make sure that each one is a different color.

- Glue the assembled continents, two hands holding the world, and the last verse onto the backboard.

- Attach the name of each continent to a manipulative piece and to the grouped continents on the backboard.

- Glue a hand to each book page.

- After everything has been laminated, attach the receiving end of Velcro to each hand and the other piece of Velcro to the back of the manipulative.

Continents
Tune: He's Got the Whole World
in His Hands

Title page

I've got North America in my hands,
I've got North America in my hands,
I've got North America in my hands,
Now I can find where it goes.

First verse — **Manipulative piece**

I've got South America in my hands,
I've got South America in my hands,
I've got South America in my hands,
Now I can find where it goes.

Second verse — **Manipulative piece**

I've got Europe in my hands,
I've got Europe in my hands,
I've got Europe in my hands,
Now I can find where it goes.

Third verse — **Manipulative piece**

I've got Asia in my hands,
I've got Asia in my hands,
I've got Asia in my hands,
Now I can find where it goes.

Fourth verse — **Manipulative piece**

I've got Africa in my hands,
I've got Africa in my hands,
I've got Africa in my hands,
Now I can find where it goes.

Fifth verse — **Manipulative piece**

CONTINENTS

Tune: He's Got the Whole World in His Hands

I've got Australia in my hands,
I've got Australia in my hands,
I've got Australia in my hands,
Now I can find where it goes.

Sixth verse   **Manipulative piece**

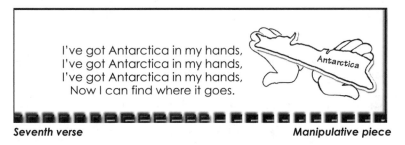

I've got Antarctica in my hands,
I've got Antarctica in my hands,
I've got Antarctica in my hands,
Now I can find where it goes.

Seventh verse   **Manipulative piece**

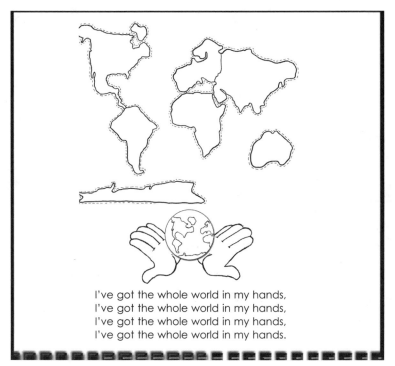

I've got the whole world in my hands,
I've got the whole world in my hands,
I've got the whole world in my hands,
I've got the whole world in my hands.

Backboard with last verse

I've got North America in my hands,
I've got North America in my hands,
I've got North America in my hands,
Now I can find where it goes.

I've got South America in my hands,
I've got South America in my hands,
I've got South America in my hands,
Now I can find where it goes.

I've got Africa in my hands,
I've got Africa in my hands,
I've got Africa in my hands,
Now I can find where it goes.

I've got Europe in my hands,
I've got Europe in my hands,
I've got Europe in my hands,
Now I can find where it goes.

I've got Asia in my hands,
I've got Asia in my hands,
I've got Asia in my hands,
Now I can find where it goes.

I've got Australia in my hands,
I've got Australia in my hands,
I've got Australia in my hands,
Now I can find where it goes.

I've got Antarctica in my hands,
I've got Antarctica in my hands,
I've got Antarctica in my hands,
Now I can find where it goes.

I've got the whole world in my hands,
I've got the whole world in my hands,
I've got the whole world in my hands,
I've got the whole world in my hands.

Tip

Photocopy and cut out the continents from an atlas to show more information.

- Cut 7 copies of a single hand to hold a continent on each page accompanied with the text.
- Cut 1 pair of hands and the world for the backboard.

- Print or copy the continents' names 2 times:
  — 1 to label backboard pieces
  — 1 to label manipulative pieces

North America

South America

Europe

Asia

Africa

Australia

Antarctica

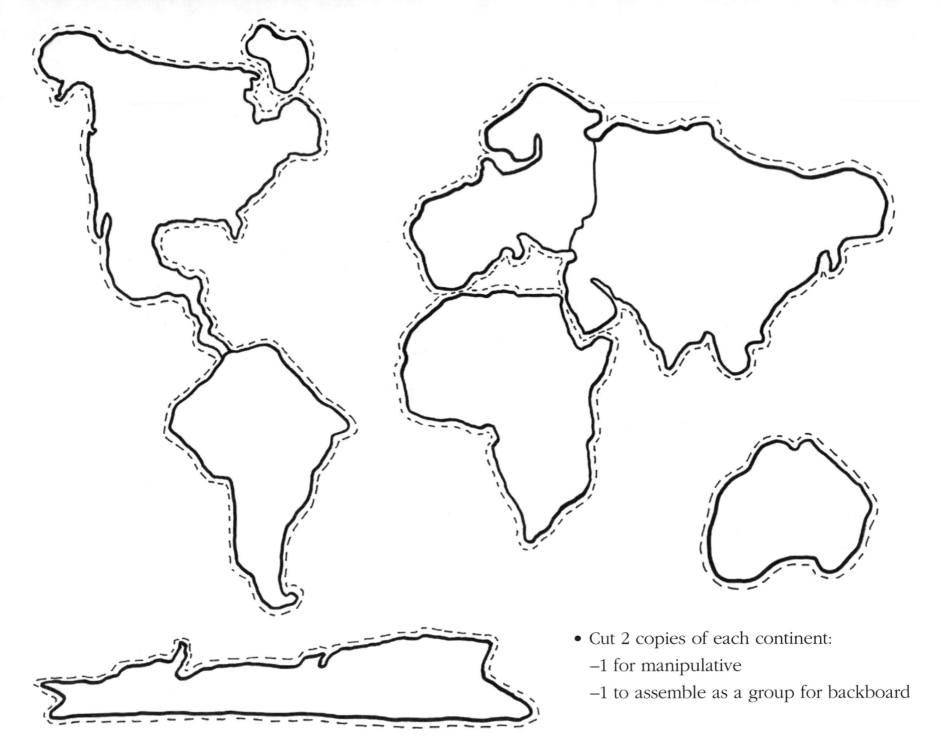

- Cut 2 copies of each continent:
  - –1 for manipulative
  - –1 to assemble as a group for backboard

COOKIE MATH

SKILL: Counting to 5

Instructions:

- Glue the glass of milk and the last verse to the backboard.

- Velcro the cookies around the glass of milk, then move them onto the glass for "dunking."

Cookie Math
Tune: London Bridge

Title page

Find the cookie with one chip,
With one chip, with one chip.
Find the cookie with one chip,
Dunk it in the milk.

First verse   *Manipulative piece*

Find the cookie with two chips,
With two chips, with two chips.
Find the cookie with two chips,
Dunk it in the milk.

Second verse   *Manipulative piece*

Find the cookie with three chips,
With three chips, with three chips.
Find the cookie with three chips,
Dunk it in the milk.

Third verse   *Manipulative piece*

Find the cookie with four chips,
With four chips, with four chips.
Find the cookie with four chips,
Dunk it in the milk.

Fourth verse   *Manipulative piece*

Find the cookie with five chips,
With five chips, with five chips.
Find the cookie with five chips,
Dunk it in the milk.

Backboard with last verse   *Manipulative piece*

COOKIE MATH

Tune: London Bridge

Find the cookie with one chip,
With one chip, with one chip.
Find the cookie with one chip,
Dunk it in the milk.

Find the cookie with two chips,
With two chips, with two chips.
Find the cookie with two chips,
Dunk it in the milk.

Find the cookie with three chips,
With three chips, with three chips.
Find the cookie with three chips,
Dunk it in the milk.

Find the cookie with four chips,
With four chips, with four chips.
Find the cookie with four chips,
Dunk it in the milk.

Find the cookie with five chips,
With five chips, with five chips.
Find the cookie with five chips,
Dunk it in the milk.

Tip

As a variation, decorate the cookies with M&Ms, raisins, or nuts instead of chocolate chips. Just remember to change the words to the song from "chips" to "bits" or "nuts."

- Cut out 1 of each cookie.
- Cut out 1 glass of milk.

COUNTING PENNIES

Instructions:

- Glue the pig and the last verse to the backboard.
- Mark an "x" where the manipulatives should be placed on the piggy bank.

Counting Pennies
Tune: Ten Little Indians

Title page

One little, two little, three little pennies,

First verse   **Manipulative pieces**

Four little, five little, six little pennies,

Second verse   **Manipulative pieces**

Seven little, eight little, nine little pennies,

Third verse   **Manipulative pieces**

Ten little pennies make a dime.

Backboard with last verse   **Manipulative pieces**

COUNTING PENNIES

Tune: Ten Little Indians

One little, two little,
three little pennies,

Four little, five little,
six little pennies,

Seven little, eight little,
nine little pennies,

Ten little pennies make a dime.

Tip

Use real coins with Velcro attached to them.

- Cut out 10 pennies.
- Cut out 1 dime.

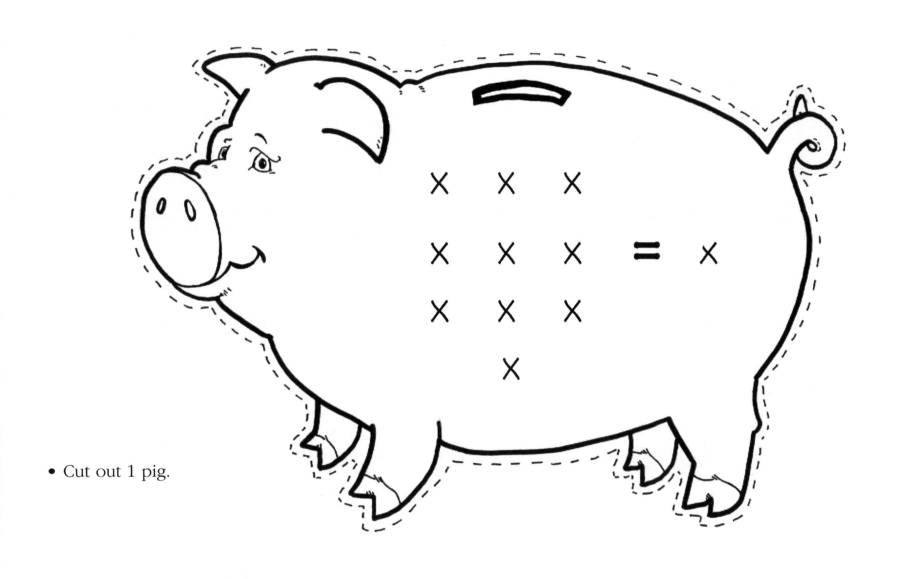

• Cut out 1 pig.

CRAYON BOX

Instructions:

- Use a large, 10" x 13" manila envelope for the backboard and decorate it to look like a crayon box with a flip top.

- Make the title/tune page so that it looks like part of the crayon box.

- Write, highlight, or underline color words with the appropriate colored marker.

- Place each crayon inside the box when you sing the verse with its color.

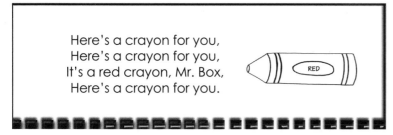

Crayon Box

Tune: Happy Birthday

Title page

Here's a crayon for you,
Here's a crayon for you,
It's a red crayon, Mr. Box,
Here's a crayon for you.

RED

First verse   *Manipulative piece*

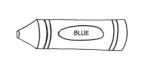

Here's a crayon for you,
Here's a crayon for you,
It's a blue crayon, Mr. Box,
Here's a crayon for you.

BLUE

Second verse   *Manipulative piece*

Here's a crayon for you,
Here's a crayon for you,
It's a yellow crayon, Mr. Box,
Here's a crayon for you.

YELLOW

Third verse   *Manipulative piece*

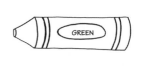

Here's a crayon for you,
Here's a crayon for you,
It's a green crayon, Mr. Box,
Here's a crayon for you.

GREEN

Fourth verse   *Manipulative piece*

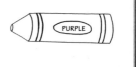

Here's a crayon for you,
Here's a crayon for you,
It's a purple crayon, Mr. Box,
Here's a crayon for you.

PURPLE

Fifth verse   *Manipulative piece*

Here's a crayon for you,
Here's a crayon for you,
It's an orange crayon, Mr. Box,
Here's a crayon for you.

ORANGE

Sixth verse   *Manipulative piece*

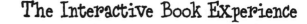

Here's a crayon for you,
Here's a crayon for you,
It's a brown crayon, Mr. Box,
Here's a crayon for you.

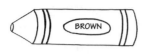

Seventh verse   **Manipulative piece**

Here's a crayon for you,
Here's a crayon for you,
It's a black crayon, Mr. Box,
Here's a crayon for you.

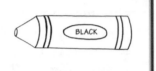

Eighth verse   **Manipulative piece**

I'll put the lid on for you,
I'll put the lid on for you,
It's time to close your top,
I'll put the lid on for you.

Backboard with last verse

CRAYON BOX

Tune: Happy Birthday

Here's a crayon for you,

Here's a crayon for you,

It's a red crayon, Mr. Box,

Here's a crayon for you.

Here's a crayon for you,

Here's a crayon for you,

It's a blue crayon, Mr. Box,

Here's a crayon for you.

Here's a crayon for you,

Here's a crayon for you,

It's a yellow crayon, Mr. Box,

Here's a crayon for you.

Here's a crayon for you,
Here's a crayon for you,
It's a green crayon, Mr. Box,
Here's a crayon for you.

Here's a crayon for you,
Here's a crayon for you,
It's a purple crayon, Mr. Box,
Here's a crayon for you.

Here's a crayon for you,
Here's a crayon for you,
It's an orange crayon, Mr. Box,
Here's a crayon for you.

Here's a crayon for you,
Here's a crayon for you,
It's a brown crayon, Mr. Box,
Here's a crayon for you.

Here's a crayon for you,
Here's a crayon for you,
It's a black crayon, Mr. Box,
Here's a crayon for you.

I'll put the lid on for you,
I'll put the lid on for you,
It's time to close your top,
I'll put the lid on for you.

Tip

Use real crayons for manipulatives.

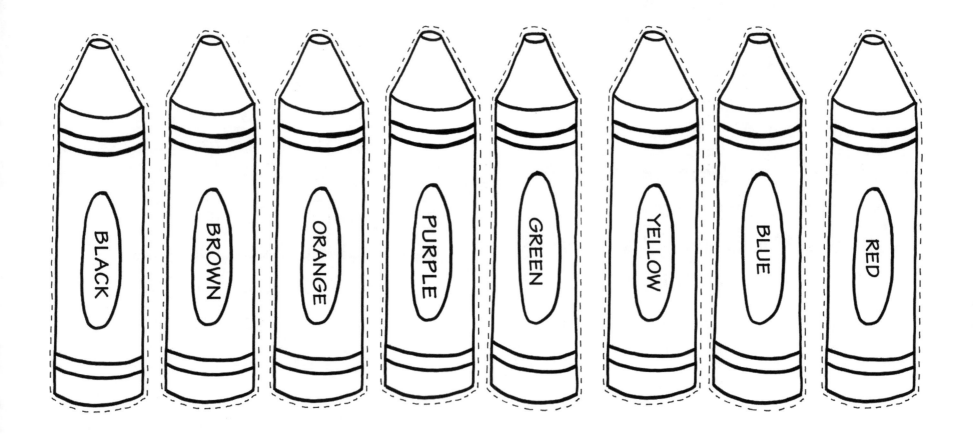

- Cut 2 crayons for each color:
  - 1 for manipulative
  - 1 for book page

DINOSAUR BONES

Instructions:

- Assemble the dinosaur and trace around the outside of it onto colored construction paper. Cut out the shape and glue it to the backboard.

Dinosaur Bones
Tune: Dem Bones

Title page

The head bone's connected to the...

First verse *Manipulative piece*

. . . neck bone.
The neck bone's connected to the...

Second verse *Manipulative piece*

. . . backbone.
The backbone's connected to the...

Third verse *Manipulative piece*

. . . hip bone.
The hip bone's connected to the...

Fourth verse *Manipulative piece*

. . . tailbone.
The tailbone's connected.
Make a T-Rex!

Backboard with last verse *Manipulative piece*

Dinosaur Bones

Tune: Dem Bones

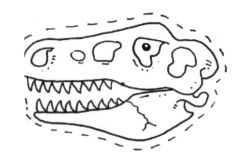

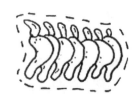

The head bone's connected to
the... neck bone.

The neck bone's connected to
the... backbone.

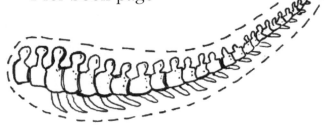

The backbone's connected to
the... hip bone.

- Cut 2 of each set of
  bones:
    — 1 for manipulative
    — 1 for book page

The hip bone's connected to the...
tailbone.

The tailbone's connected.
Make a T-Rex!

EGGS IN A BASKET

SKILLS: Colors and color words

Instructions:

- Assemble the basket and glue to the backboard along with the last verse.

- Highlight color words with the appropriate colored marker.

Eggs in a Basket
Tune: A Tisket, A Tasket

Title page

A tisket, a tasket,
Put your eggs in my basket.
A tisket, a tasket,
Put the purple egg in my basket.

First verse **Manipulative piece**

A tisket, a tasket,
Put your eggs in my basket.
A tisket, a tasket,
Put the green egg in my basket.

Second verse **Manipulative piece**

A tisket, a tasket,
Put your eggs in my basket.
A tisket, a tasket,
Put the black egg in my basket.

Third verse **Manipulative piece**

A tisket, a tasket,
Put your eggs in my basket.
A tisket, a tasket,
Put the yellow egg in my basket.

Fourth verse **Manipulative piece**

A tisket, a tasket,
Put your eggs in my basket.
A tisket, a tasket,
Put the pink egg in my basket.

Fifth verse **Manipulative piece**

A tisket, a tasket,
Put your eggs in my basket.
A tisket, a tasket,
Put the blue egg in my basket.

Sixth verse **Manipulative piece**

A tisket, a tasket,
Put your eggs in my basket.
A tisket, a tasket,
Put the white egg in my basket.

Seventh verse   *Manipulative piece*

A tisket, a tasket,
Put your eggs in my basket.
A tisket, a tasket,
Put the red egg in my basket.

Eighth verse   *Manipulative piece*

A tisket, a tasket,
Put your eggs in my basket.
A tisket, a tasket,
Put the brown egg in my basket.

Ninth verse   *Manipulative piece*

A tisket, a tasket,
Put your eggs in my basket.
A tisket, a tasket,
Put the orange egg in my basket.

Tenth verse   *Manipulative piece*

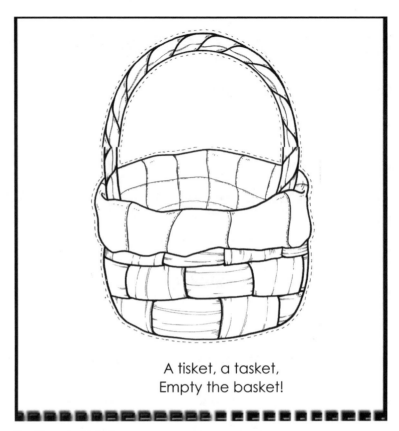

A tisket, a tasket,
Empty the basket!

Backboard with last verse

Eggs in a Basket

Tune: A Tisket, A Tasket

A tisket, a tasket,
Put your eggs in my basket.
A tisket, a tasket,
Put the yellow egg in my basket.

A tisket, a tasket,
Put your eggs in my basket.
A tisket, a tasket,
Put the purple egg in my basket.

A tisket, a tasket,
Put your eggs in my basket.
A tisket, a tasket,
Put the pink egg in my basket.

A tisket, a tasket,
Put your eggs in my basket.
A tisket, a tasket,
Put the green egg in my basket.

A tisket, a tasket,
Put your eggs in my basket.
A tisket, a tasket,
Put the blue egg in my basket.

A tisket, a tasket,
Put your eggs in my basket.
A tisket, a tasket,
Put the black egg in my basket.

A tisket, a tasket,
Put your eggs in my basket.
A tisket, a tasket,
Put the white egg in my basket.

A tisket, a tasket,
Put your eggs in my basket.
A tisket, a tasket,
Put the red egg in my basket.

A tisket, a tasket,
Put your eggs in my basket.
A tisket, a tasket,
Put the brown egg in my basket.

A tisket, a tasket,
Put your eggs in my basket.
A tisket, a tasket,
Put the orange egg in my basket.

A tisket, a tasket,
Empty the basket!

• Cut 20 eggs, 2 for each color:
— 1 for manipulative
— 1 for book page

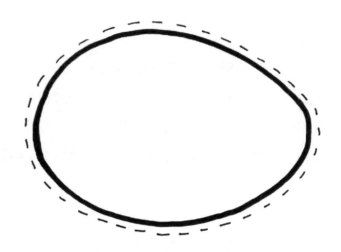

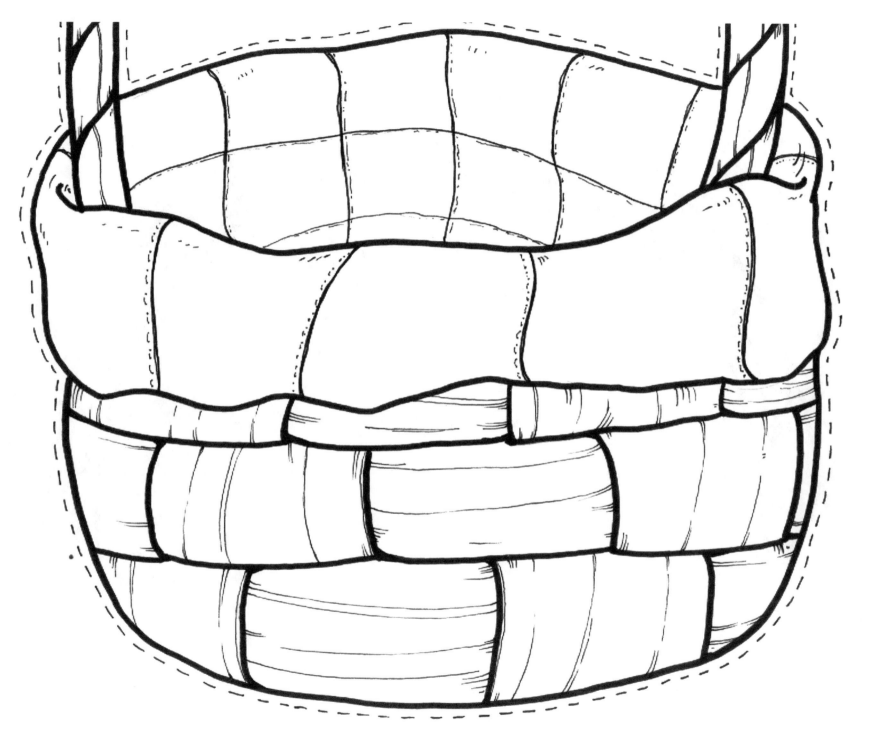

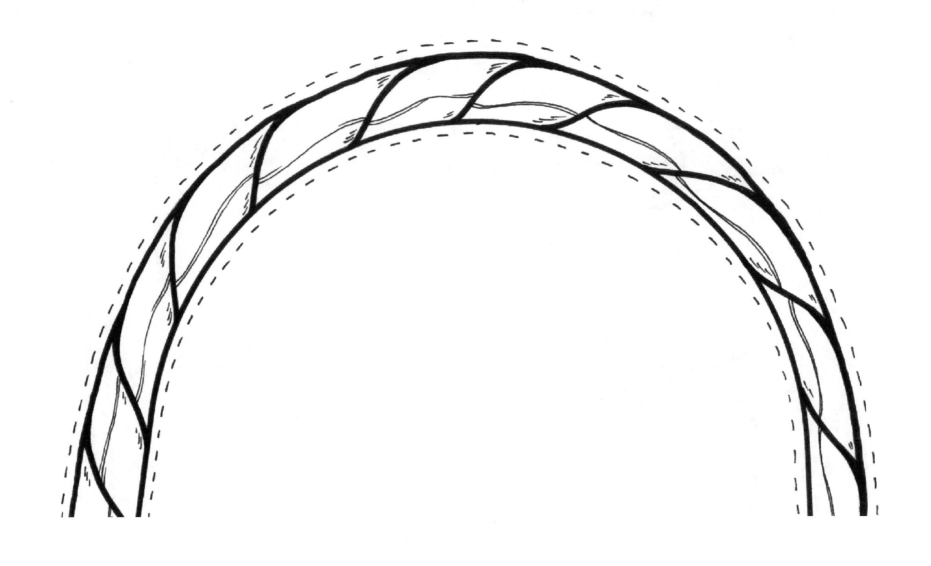

HEY! I CAN READ THIS!

FIVE LITTLE CHILDREN

SKILLS: Counting to 5, backward and forward

Instructions:

- To begin this book, the manipulative pieces should be on the backboard. Then they are moved from the bed and onto the book pages as each verse is sung—and each child falls off. At the end of the song, students return the pieces to the backboard, counting forward from 1 to 5.

- Cut the pillow and blanket separately from different colors of construction paper.

Five Little Children

Tune: Five Little Monkeys
(Note: Sing the pronoun that matches the gender of the child pictured.)

Title page

---

5 little children jumping on the bed.
1 fell off and bumped her head.
Mama called the doctor and the doctor said,
"No more children jumping on the bed!"

First verse · *Manipulative piece*

---

4 little children jumping on the bed.
1 fell off and bumped her head.
Mama called the doctor and the doctor said,
"No more children jumping on the bed!"

Second verse · *Manipulative piece*

---

3 little children jumping on the bed.
1 fell off and bumped his head.
Mama called the doctor and the doctor said,
"No more children jumping on the bed!"

Third verse · *Manipulative piece*

---

2 little children jumping on the bed.
1 fell off and bumped his head.
Mama called the doctor and the doctor said,
"No more children jumping on the bed!"

Fourth verse · *Manipulative piece*

1 little child was jumping on the bed.
She fell off and bumped her head.
Mama called the doctor and the doctor said,
"Put those children back in bed!"

Backboard with last verse   *Manipulative piece*

FIVE LITTLE CHILDREN

Tune: Five Little Monkeys

(Note: Sing the pronoun that matches the gender of the child pictured.)

5 little children jumping on the bed.

1 fell off and bumped her head.

Mama called the doctor and the doctor said,

"No more children jumping on the bed!"

4 little children jumping on the bed.

1 fell off and bumped her head.

Mama called the doctor and the doctor said,

"No more children jumping on the bed!"

3 little children jumping on the bed.

1 fell off and bumped his head.

Mama called the doctor and the doctor said,

"No more children jumping on the bed!"

2 little children jumping on the bed.

1 fell off and bumped his head.

Mama called the doctor and the doctor said,

"No more children jumping on the bed!"

1 little child was jumping on the bed.

She fell off and bumped her head.

Mama called the doctor and the doctor said,

"Put those children back in bed!"

• Cut 1 bed for the backboard.

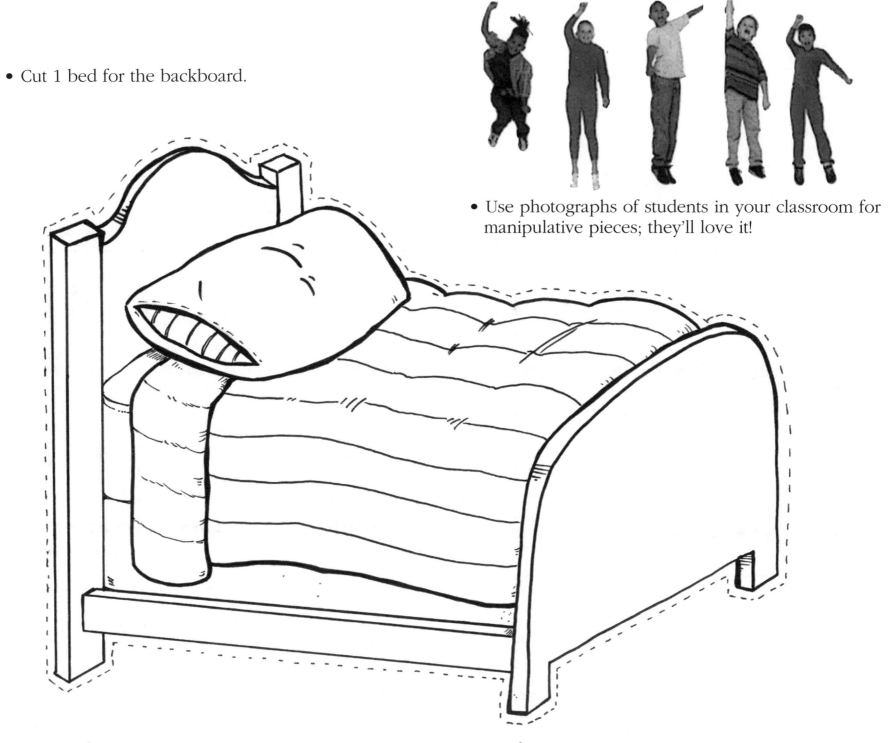

• Use photographs of students in your classroom for manipulative pieces; they'll love it!

GERMS

Instructions:

- This book is different in that the manipulative pieces don't match the ones glued to the page. Read the text to note placement.

Germs
Tune: Happy Birthday

Title page

Germs make you sick,
They're around everywhere,
You can't see them,
But you need to know they're there.

First verse   *Manipulative piece*

Here's a fever germ,
Here's a fever germ,
It's hiding on the crayon,
Here's a fever germ.

Second verse   *Manipulative piece*

Here's a stomachache germ,
Here's a stomachache germ,
It's hiding on the puzzle piece,
Here's a stomachache germ.

Third verse   *Manipulative piece*

Here's a runny nose germ,
Here's a runny nose germ,
It's hiding on the block,
Here's a runny nose germ.

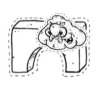

Fourth verse   *Manipulative piece*

Here's a sore throat germ,
Here's a sore throat germ,
It's hiding on the play food,
Here's a sore throat germ.

Fifth verse   *Manipulative piece*

Here's a headache germ,
Here's a headache germ,
It's hiding on the play dough,
Here's a headache germ.

Sixth verse   *Manipulative piece*

GERMS

Tune: Happy Birthday

Germs are on your hands,
And they'll make you sick,
Use lots of soap and water,
And get rid of the germs quick!

Backboard with last verse   *Manipulative piece*

Germs make you sick,
They're around everywhere,
You can't see them,
But you need to know they're there.

Here's a fever germ,
Here's a fever germ,
It's hiding on the crayon,
Here's a fever germ.

Here's a stomachache germ,
Here's a stomachache germ,
It's hiding on the puzzle piece,
Here's a stomachache germ.

Tip

Trace a child's hands for the backboard.

Here's a runny nose germ,
Here's a runny nose germ,
It's hiding on the block,
Here's a runny nose germ.

Here's a sore throat germ,
Here's a sore throat germ,
It's hiding on the play food,
Here's a sore throat germ.

Here's a headache germ,
Here's a headache germ,
It's hiding on the play dough,
Here's a headache germ.

Germs are on your hands,
And they'll make you sick,
Use lots of soap and water,
And get rid of the germs quick!

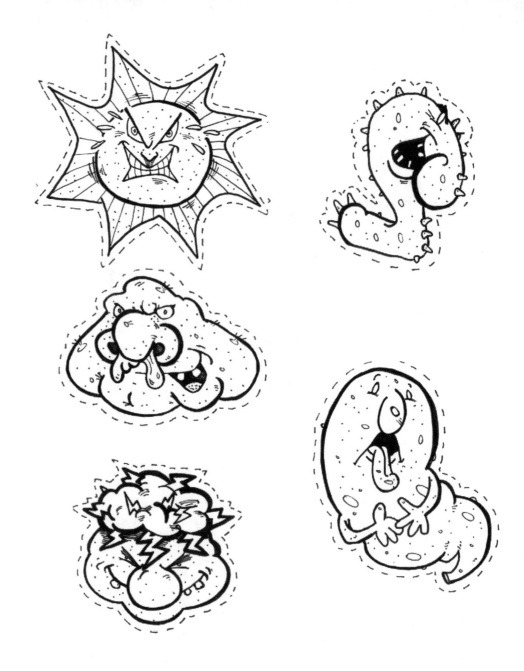

• Cut 1 of each for manipulative.

• Cut 2 soap pieces:

  –1 for manipulative
  –1 to glue on the backboard

• Cut 1 crayon, block, puzzle piece, play food, and play dough, and glue to the book pages.

• Cut 2 hands to glue on the backboard.

GIFTS

Instructions:

- This book provides a great opportunity to introduce the use of a thought bubble.

- The wrapped gift boxes, boy, and thought bubble are not manipulatives. Glue the boxes to the title page and the boy and thought bubble to the backboard.

- Place the piggy bank so it is upside down to show it is empty.

Gifts

Tune: London Bridge

Title page

I would like to be Santa,
be Santa, be Santa.
I would like to be Santa,
And give lots of gifts.

First verse   **Manipulative piece**

But I have no money, money, money.
But I have no money,
Hey – I know what I'll do!

Second verse   **Manipulative piece**

I'll make my bed to help my mom,
help my mom, help my mom.
I'll make my bed to help my mom,
so she'll know I care.

Third verse   **Manipulative piece**

I'll take the trash out for my dad,
for my dad, for my dad.
I'll take the trash out for my dad,
so he'll know I care.

Fourth verse   **Manipulative piece**

I'll read a story to the baby,
to the baby, to the baby.
I'll read a story to the baby,
so she'll know I care.

Fifth verse   **Manipulative piece**

I'll give the dog a bone to chew,
bone to chew, bone to chew.
I'll give the dog a bone to chew,
so he will know I care.

Sixth verse   **Manipulative piece**

I'll draw my teacher a picture,
picture, picture.
I'll draw my teacher a picture,
so she'll know I care.

Seventh verse   *Manipulative piece*

Making others happy makes
me feel great!

Backboard with last verse

GIFTS

Tune: London Bridge

I would like to give some gifts, give
some gifts, give some gifts.
I would like to give some gifts,
And make others happy.

But I have no money, money,
money.
But I have no money,
Hey – I know what I'll do!

I'll make my bed to help my mom,
help my mom, help my mom.
I'll make my bed to help my mom,
so she'll know I care.

I'll take the trash out for my dad,
for my dad, for my dad.
I'll take the trash out for my dad,
so he'll know I care.

I'll read a story to the baby,
to the baby, to the baby.
I'll read a story to the baby,
so she'll know I care.

I'll give the dog a bone to chew,
bone to chew, bone to chew.
I'll give the dog a bone to chew,
so he will know I care.

I'll draw my teacher a picture,
picture, picture.
I'll draw my teacher a picture,
so she'll know I care.

Making others happy makes me feel great!

• Enlarge and cut out 1 thought bubble.

- Cut 2 of each bed, bag of trash, book, bone, picture, Santa's hat, and piggy bank:
  — 1 for manipulative
  — 1 for book page

- Copy and cut out as many wrapped gift boxes as desired for the title page.

- Cut 1 boy.

Me + T

GINGERBREAD MAN

SKILLS: Counting to 10, backward and forward

Instructions:

- To begin, the 10 gingerbread men are on the book pages, then they are moved to the cookie sheet. Next, the process reverses.

- To encourage numeral matching and recognition, number each gingerbread man and the corresponding piece of Velcro.

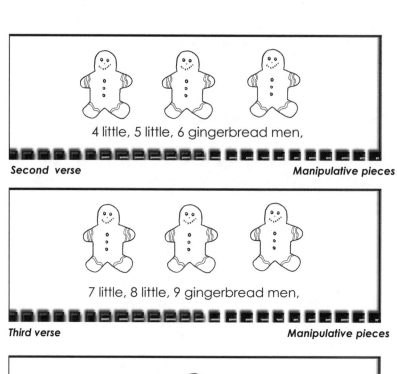

4 little, 5 little, 6 gingerbread men,

Second verse   *Manipulative pieces*

7 little, 8 little, 9 gingerbread men,

Third verse   *Manipulative pieces*

Gingerbread Man

Tune: Ten Little Indians

Title page

10 gingerbread men for us to eat!

Fourth verse   *Manipulative piece*

1 little, 2 little, 3 gingerbread men,

First verse   *Manipulative pieces*

10 gulp, 9 gulp, 8 gingerbread men,

Fifth verse   *Manipulative pieces*

7 gulp, 6 gulp, 5 gingerbread men,

Sixth verse   *Manipulative pieces*

4 gulp, 3 gulp, 2 gingerbread men,

Seventh verse   *Manipulative pieces*

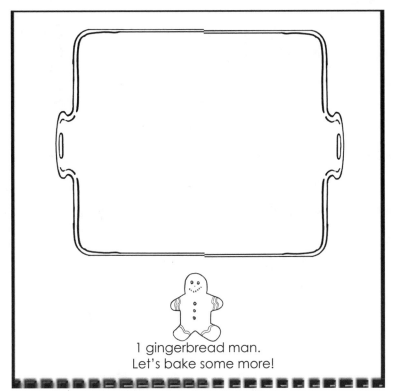

1 gingerbread man.
Let's bake some more!

Backboard with last verse

Gingerbread Man

Tune: Ten Little Indians

1 little, 2 little, 3 gingerbread men,

4 little, 5 little, 6 gingerbread men,

7 little, 8 little, 9 gingerbread men,

10 gingerbread men for us to eat!

10 gulp, 9 gulp, 8 gingerbread men,

7 gulp, 6 gulp, 5 gingerbread men,

4 gulp, 3 gulp, 2 gingerbread men,

1 gingerbread man.
Let's bake some more!

- Cut 10 gingerbread men.
- Cut 2 cookie sheets from aluminum foil and join to make a whole sheet.

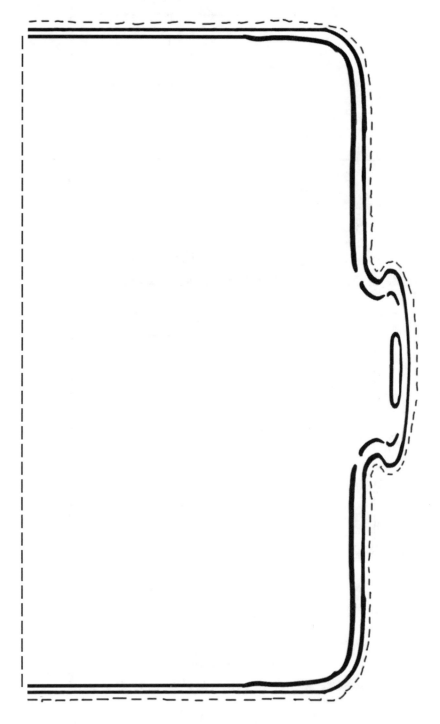

GRANDMA'S HOUSE

Instructions:

- For the backboard, draw a house in a country scene (winding road, grassy hillside, sky, clouds) and cut out the pieces from construction paper. Assemble the pieces and glue them onto the backboard. Then glue Grandma onto the bottom left-hand corner of the backboard.

- Attach one part of a piece of Velcro to various places in the country scene on the backboard where you want the manipulatives to be attached.

- Draw and color the appropriate design for the window on each car/book page.

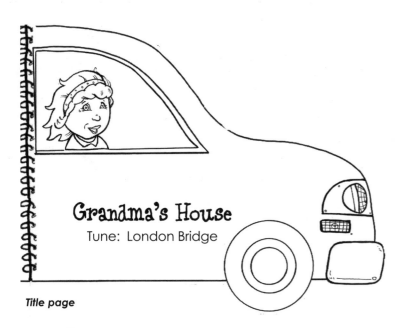

Grandma's House
Tune: London Bridge

Title page

On the way to
Grandma's house,
Grandma's house,
Grandma's house.
On the way to
Grandma's house,
This is what I saw...

First verse

A tree!

Manipulative piece

On the way to
Grandma's house,
Grandma's house,
Grandma's house.
On the way to
Grandma's house,
This is what I saw...

Second verse

A cow!

Manipulative piece

On the way to
Grandma's house,
Grandma's house,
Grandma's house.
On the way to
Grandma's house,
This is what I saw...

Third verse

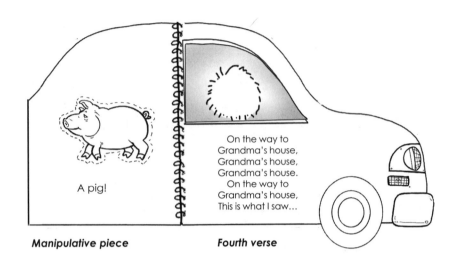

A pig!

On the way to
Grandma's house,
Grandma's house,
Grandma's house.
On the way to
Grandma's house,
This is what I saw...

Manipulative piece   **Fourth verse**

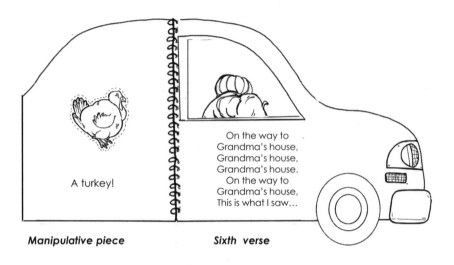

A turkey!

On the way to
Grandma's house,
Grandma's house,
Grandma's house.
On the way to
Grandma's house,
This is what I saw...

Manipulative piece   **Sixth verse**

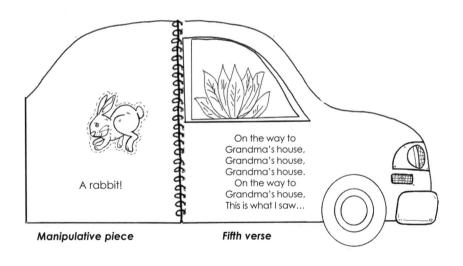

A rabbit!

On the way to
Grandma's house,
Grandma's house,
Grandma's house.
On the way to
Grandma's house,
This is what I saw...

Manipulative piece   **Fifth verse**

"Grandma!"

Backboard

Grandma's House

Tune: London Bridge

On the way to Grandma's house,
Grandma's house, Grandma's house.
On the way to Grandma's house,
This is what I saw...

A tree!

On the way to Grandma's house,
Grandma's house, Grandma's house.
On the way to Grandma's house,
This is what I saw...

A cow!

On the way to Grandma's house,
Grandma's house, Grandma's house.
On the way to Grandma's house,
This is what I saw...

A pig!

On the way to Grandma's house,
Grandma's house, Grandma's house.
On the way to Grandma's house,
This is what I saw...

A rabbit!

On the way to Grandma's house,
Grandma's house, Grandma's house.
On the way to Grandma's house,
This is what I saw...

A turkey!

Grandma!

- **Title/tune page**

  Window: Girl's face

- **First verse page**

  Window: Green background with red apples

  Opposite page: The words "A tree!" cut out and glued on

- **Second verse page**

  Window: White background with black spots

  Opposite page: The words "A cow!" cut out and glued on

- **Third verse page**

  Window: Pink background with brown spots

  Opposite page: The words "A pig!" cut out and glued on

- **Fourth verse page**

  Window: Gray background with white rabbit tail

  Opposite page: The words "A rabbit!" cut out and glued on

- **Fifth verse page**

  Window: Brown background with colored feathers

  Opposite page: The words "A turkey!" cut out and glued on

- **Backboard:** Grandma and the word "Grandma!" cut out and glued on

- Cut 1 rabbit, turkey, cow, pig, and tree for manipulatives.

- Cut 6 copies of car for book pages.

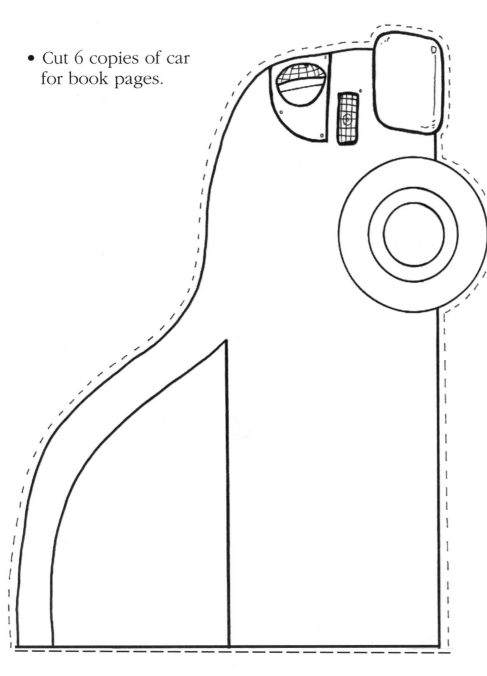

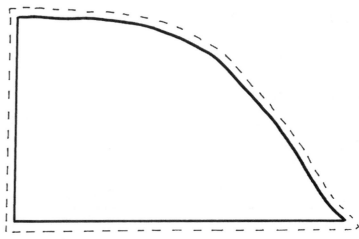

- Cut 6 window pieces and attach 1 to each car page.

- Cut 1 girl for the car window on the title/tune page.

- Cut 1 Grandma and glue on the backboard.

HONEYBEE SONG

Instructions:

- To promote numeral recognition, number the bees.
- Glue the hive, 1 bee, and the last verse to the backboard.

Honeybee Song
Tune: One Elephant Went Out to Play

Title page

---

1 honeybee went out to play,
Upon a beehive one day.
He had so very, very much fun,
That he buzzed for another little
honeybee to come.

First verse   *Manipulative piece*

---

2 honeybees went out to play,
Upon a beehive one day.
They had so very, very much fun,
That they buzzed for another little
honeybee to come.

Second verse   *Manipulative piece*

---

3 honeybees went out to play,
Upon a beehive one day.
They had so very, very much fun,
That they buzzed for another little
honeybee to come.

Third verse   *Manipulative piece*

---

4 honeybees went out to play,
Upon a beehive one day.
They had so very, very much fun,
That they buzzed for another little
honeybee to come.

Fourth verse   *Manipulative piece*

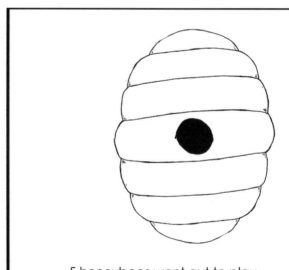

5 honeybees went out to play,
Upon a beehive one day.
They had so very, very much fun,
That they all got tired and went
home to their moms.

Backboard with last verse   *Manipulative piece*

Honeybee Song

Tune: One Elephant Went Out to Play

1 honeybee went out to play,
Upon a beehive one day.
He had so very, very much fun,
That he buzzed for another little
honeybee to come.

2 honeybees went out to play,
Upon a beehive one day.
They had so very, very much fun,
That they buzzed for another little
honeybee to come.

3 honeybees went out to play,
Upon a beehive one day.
They had so very, very much fun,
That they buzzed for another little
honeybee to come.

4 honeybees went out to play,
Upon a beehive one day.
They had so very, very much fun,
That they buzzed for another little
honeybee to come.

5 honeybees went out to play,
Upon a beehive one day.
They had so very, very much fun,
That they all got tired and went
home to their moms.

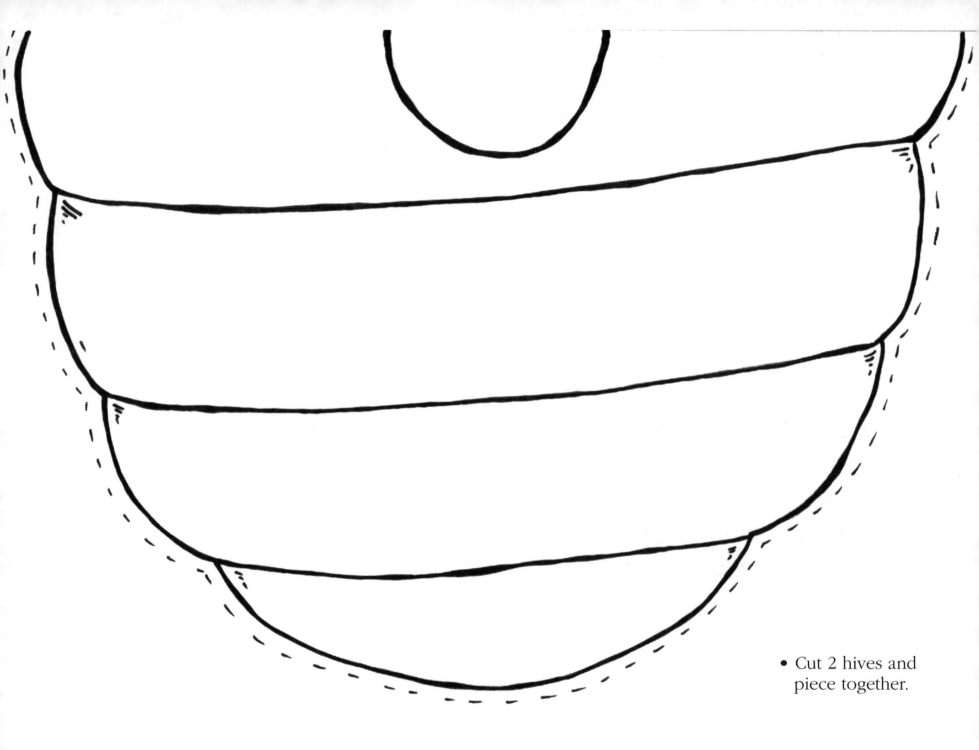

• Cut 2 hives and piece together.

- Cut 2 of each bee:
    - 1 for manipulative
    - 1 for each book page

Tips

**Use wiggly eyes on some of the bees.
Use glitter on their wings.**

Mama Bird's Eggs

SKILLS: Colors and color words

Instructions:

- Glue the bird and birdhouse to the backboard so that the top of the roof and part of the bird's wings and tail feathers extend beyond the edges of the backboard.

- Glue the last nest to the backboard below the birdhouse.

- Color the eggs in the nests and the egg manipulatives to match the color word on each page.

- Glue the one verse, which is sung repeatedly, to the backboard so that it is between the bird and the egg manipulatives.

- Arrange the pages in any order you wish. They can be bound on the bottom or along the left-hand side.

- The book begins with the egg manipulatives in place on the right-hand side of the backboard.

Mama Bird's Eggs
Tune: Mary Had a Little Lamb

Title page

white

Book page

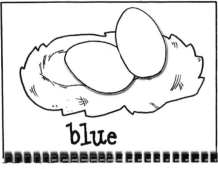

blue

Book page

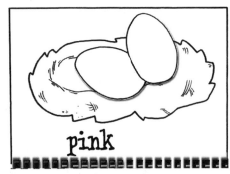

pink

Book page

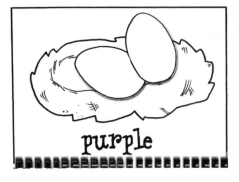

purple

Book page

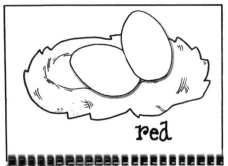

red

Book page

HEY! I CAN READ THIS!

Mama Bird has lost an egg,
Lost an egg, lost an egg.
Mama Bird has lost an egg,
Please, help her find it.

Home Tweet Home

yellow

Backboard with verse, birdhouse, nest   **Manipulative pieces**

Mama Bird's Eggs

Tune: Mary Had a Little Lamb

Mama Bird has lost an egg,
Lost an egg, lost an egg.
Mama Bird has lost an egg,
Please, help her find it.

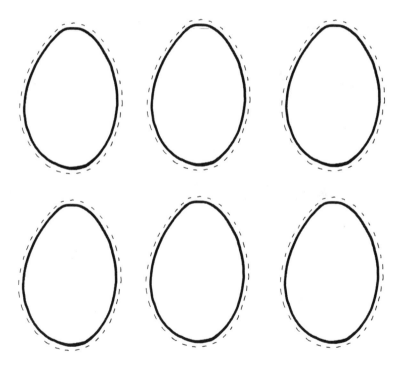

• Cut 6 eggs for manipulatives.

Tip

Write, highlight, or underline color words with the appropriate colored marker.

• Cut 1 birdhouse with bird.

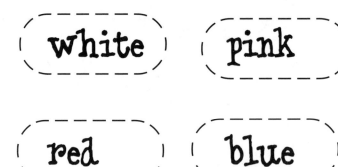

white   pink

red   blue

purple   yellow

• Cut 1 of each color word for the book pages.
• Cut 6 nests with colored eggs for the book pages.

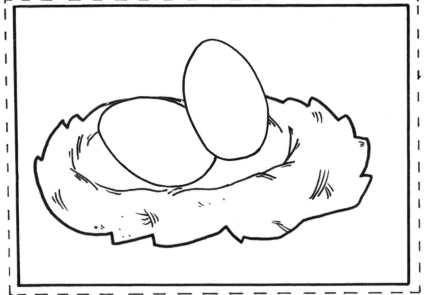

Mr. Toolbox

Instructions:

- When making the backboard, cut it out so there's a handle shape at the top.
- Trace the shape of each tool onto the backboard.
- Glue the last verse onto the backboard.

Mr. Toolbox

Tune: Are You Sleeping?

Title page

Mr. Toolbox, Mr. Toolbox,
Where are your tools?
Where are your tools?
Can you find a wrench?
Can you find a wrench?
In your box, in your box.

First verse   *Manipulative piece*

Mr. Toolbox, Mr. Toolbox,
Where are your tools?
Where are your tools?
Can you find a hammer?
Can you find a hammer?
In your box, in your box.

Second verse   *Manipulative piece*

Mr. Toolbox, Mr. Toolbox,
Where are your tools?
Where are your tools?
Can you find a tape measure?
Can you find a tape measure?
In your box, in your box.

Third verse   *Manipulative piece*

Mr. Toolbox, Mr. Toolbox,
Where are your tools?
Where are your tools?
Can you find a saw?
Can you find a saw?
In your box, in your box.

Fourth verse   *Manipulative piece*

Mr. Toolbox, Mr. Toolbox,
Where are your tools?
Where are your tools?
Can you find the pliers?
Can you find the pliers?
In your box, in your box.

Fifth verse   *Manipulative piece*

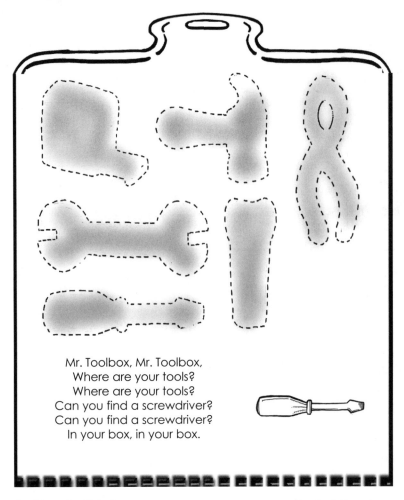

Mr. Toolbox, Mr. Toolbox,
Where are your tools?
Where are your tools?
Can you find a screwdriver?
Can you find a screwdriver?
In your box, in your box.

Backboard with last verse

Manipulative piece

Tip

Use tool pieces from a toy play set for manipulatives.

Mr. Toolbox

Tune: Are You Sleeping?

Mr. Toolbox, Mr. Toolbox,
Where are your tools?
Where are your tools?
Can you find a wrench?
Can you find a wrench?
In your box, in your box.

Mr. Toolbox, Mr. Toolbox,
Where are your tools?
Where are your tools?
Can you find a hammer?
Can you find a hammer?
In your box, in your box.

Mr. Toolbox, Mr. Toolbox,
Where are your tools?
Where are your tools?
Can you find a tape measure?
Can you find a tape measure?
In your box, in your box.

Mr. Toolbox, Mr. Toolbox,
Where are your tools?
Where are your tools?
Can you find a saw?
Can you find a saw?
In your box, in your box.

Mr. Toolbox, Mr. Toolbox,
Where are your tools?
Where are your tools?
Can you find the pliers?
Can you find the pliers?
In your box, in your box.

Mr. Toolbox, Mr. Toolbox,
Where are your tools?
Where are your tools?
Can you find a screwdriver?
Can you find a screwdriver?
In your box, in your box.

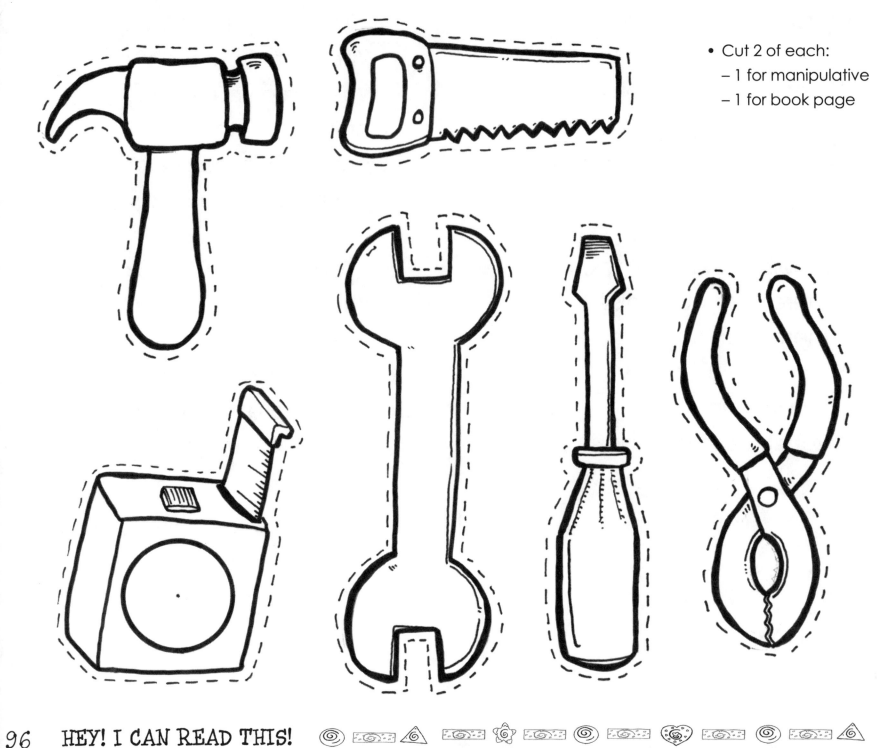

• Cut 2 of each:
 – 1 for manipulative
 – 1 for book page

HEY! I CAN READ THIS!

Ms. Square

SKILLS: Shapes and shape words

Instructions:

- The backboard for our book measures 12 inches square.
- Glue 2 teeth to each mouth.
- Glue the last verse to the backboard.
- You could use this basic idea and the same tune for books with other shapes too: triangle, rectangle, circle.

Here is one nose for you,
Here is one nose for you,
It's a circle nose, Ms. Square,
Here is one nose for you.

Second verse   *Manipulative piece*

Here are two teeth for you,
Here are two teeth for you,
They are rectangle teeth, Ms. Square,
Here are two teeth for you.

Third verse   *Manipulative piece*

Ms. Square
Tune: Happy Birthday

Title page

Here are two eyes for you,
Here are two eyes for you,
They are triangle eyes, Ms. Square,
Here are two eyes for you.

First verse   *Manipulative piece*

X   X

X

X

There are four sides to you,
There are four sides to you,
They are the same size, Ms. Square,
There are four sides to you.

```
   1
4     2
   3
```

Backboard with last verse   *Manipulative piece*

Ms. Square

Tune: Happy Birthday

Here are two eyes for you,
Here are two eyes for you,
They are triangle eyes, Ms. Square,
Here are two eyes for you.

Here is one nose for you,
Here is one nose for you,
It's a circle nose, Ms. Square,
Here is one nose for you.

Here are two teeth for you,
Here are two teeth for you,
They are rectangle teeth, Ms. Square,
Here are two teeth for you.

There are four sides to you,
There are four sides to you,
They are the same size, Ms. Square,
There are four sides to you.

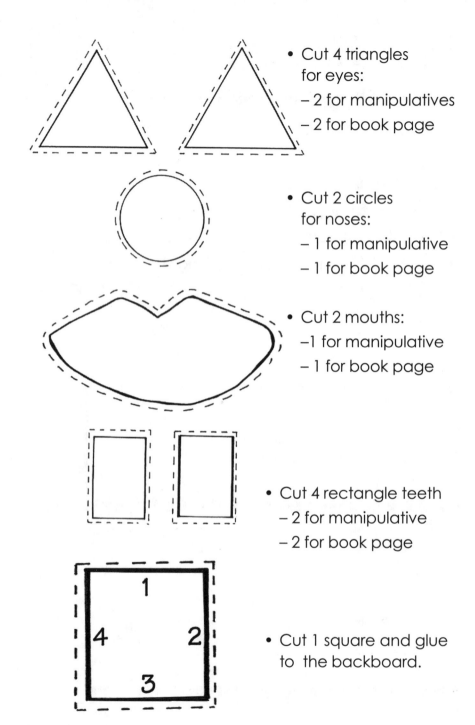

• Cut 4 triangles
  for eyes:
  – 2 for manipulatives
  – 2 for book page

• Cut 2 circles
  for noses:
  – 1 for manipulative
  – 1 for book page

• Cut 2 mouths:
  –1 for manipulative
  – 1 for book page

• Cut 4 rectangle teeth
  – 2 for manipulative
  – 2 for book page

• Cut 1 square and glue
  to the backboard.

MY NEW PUPPY

SKILL: Character education

Instructions:

- Glue the last verse to the backboard, along with the boy, tree, doghouse, clouds, grass, and heart shape.

My New Puppy

Tune: London Bridge

Title page

I just got a new puppy,
new puppy, new puppy.
I just got a new puppy,
I'll take care of him, you'll see.

First verse *Manipulative piece*

I'll give him water and food,
water and food, water and food.
I'll give him water and food,
So he will grow real good.

Second verse *Manipulative piece*

We'll play fetch with a ball,
with a ball, with a ball.
We'll play fetch with a ball,
He'll bring it when I call.

Third verse *Manipulative piece*

I will pooper scoop the yard,
scoop the yard, scoop the yard.
I will pooper scoop the yard,
Though that job's yucky and hard.

Fourth verse *Manipulative piece*

I will be his family,
family, family.
I will be his family
And he will always love me!

Backboard with last verse *Manipulative piece*

My New Puppy

Tune: London Bridge

I just got a new puppy,
new puppy, new puppy.
I just got a new puppy,
I'll take care of him, you'll see.

I'll give him water and food,
water and food, water and food.
I'll give him water and food,
So he will grow real good.

We'll play fetch with a ball,
with a ball, with a ball.
We'll play fetch with a ball,
He'll bring it when I call.

I will pooper scoop the yard,
scoop the yard, scoop the yard.
I will pooper scoop the yard,
Though that job's yucky and hard.

I will be his family,
family, family.
I will be his family
And he will always love me!

Tip

Instead of using the reproducibles provided, you could draw and color your own background on the backboard, such as a palm tree and a doghouse with a thatched roof, or whatever your imagination brings to mind.

- Cut 1 boy, tree, doghouse, grass, and clouds.
- Cut 2 of the dog, food dish, soccer ball, pooper scooper, and heart:
  - –1 for manipulative
  - –1 for book page

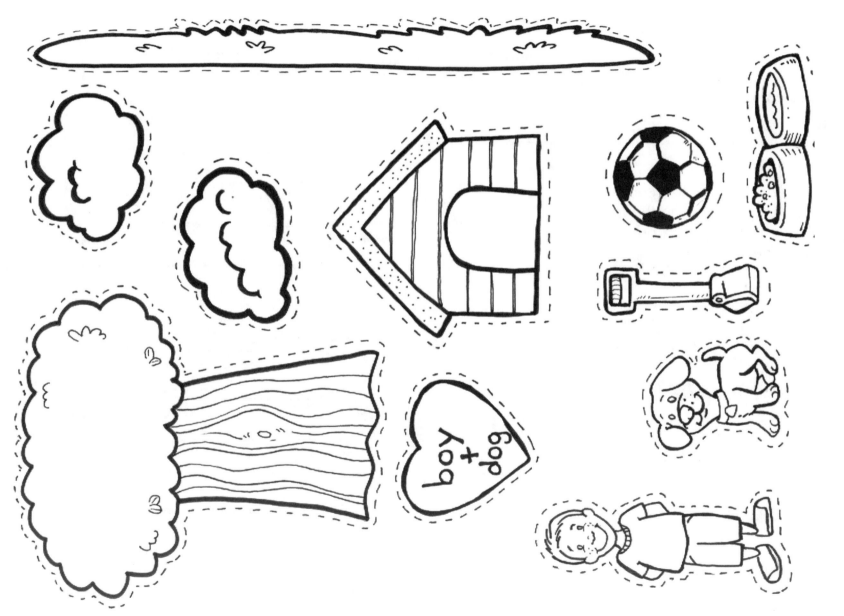

My Purse

Instructions:

- With the purse open, the book pages are arranged along the bottom right-hand side of the purse and bound along their left edge where the two halves of the purse are bound.

- Glue one set of the purse's contents and the last verse of the song to the purse in its opened position (see p. 103).

- When using the book, begin with the purse in a closed position and sing the first verse, which is glued to the front of the purse. Then open the purse and sing the next verse.

My Purse
Tune: Farmer in the Dell

The things in my purse,
The things in my purse,
Oh, how I need all the things In
my purse.

Front of book with title and first verse

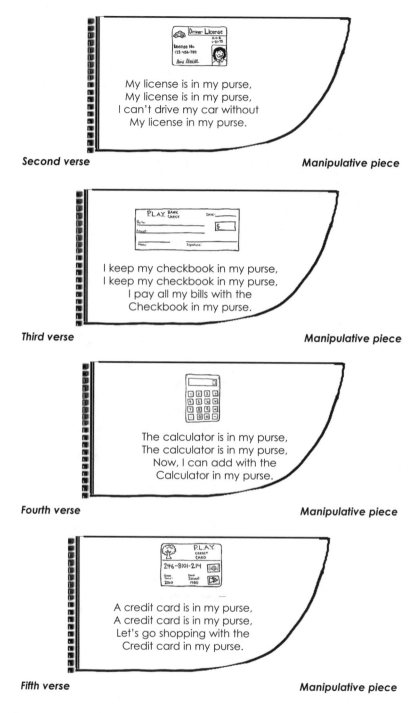

My license is in my purse,
My license is in my purse,
I can't drive my car without
My license in my purse.

Second verse   *Manipulative piece*

I keep my checkbook in my purse,
I keep my checkbook in my purse,
I pay all my bills with the
Checkbook in my purse.

Third verse   *Manipulative piece*

The calculator is in my purse,
The calculator is in my purse,
Now, I can add with the
Calculator in my purse.

Fourth verse   *Manipulative piece*

A credit card is in my purse,
A credit card is in my purse,
Let's go shopping with the
Credit card in my purse.

Fifth verse   *Manipulative piece*

My Purse

Tune: Farmer in the Dell

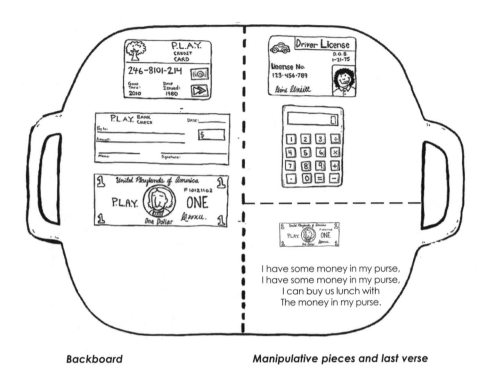

Backboard **Manipulative pieces and last verse**

The things in my purse,
The things in my purse,
Oh, how I need all the things
In my purse.

My license is in my purse,
My license is in my purse,
I can't drive my car without
My license in my purse.

I keep my checkbook in my purse,
I keep my checkbook in my purse,
I pay all my bills with the
Checkbook in my purse.

Tip

Use a play set found at a Dollar Store for manipulative pieces.

The calculator is in my purse,
The calculator is in my purse,
Now, I can add with the
Calculator in my purse.

A credit card is in my purse,
A credit card is in my purse,
Let's go shopping with the
Credit card in my purse.

I have some money in my purse,
I have some money in my purse,
I can buy us lunch with
The money in my purse.

- Cut 3 copies of each:
  – 1 for manipulative
  – 1 for backboard
  – 1 for book page

- Based on the purse size, cut 4 book pages to fit inside the purse.

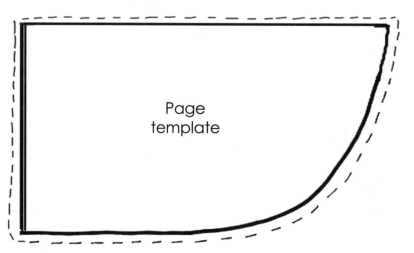

Page template

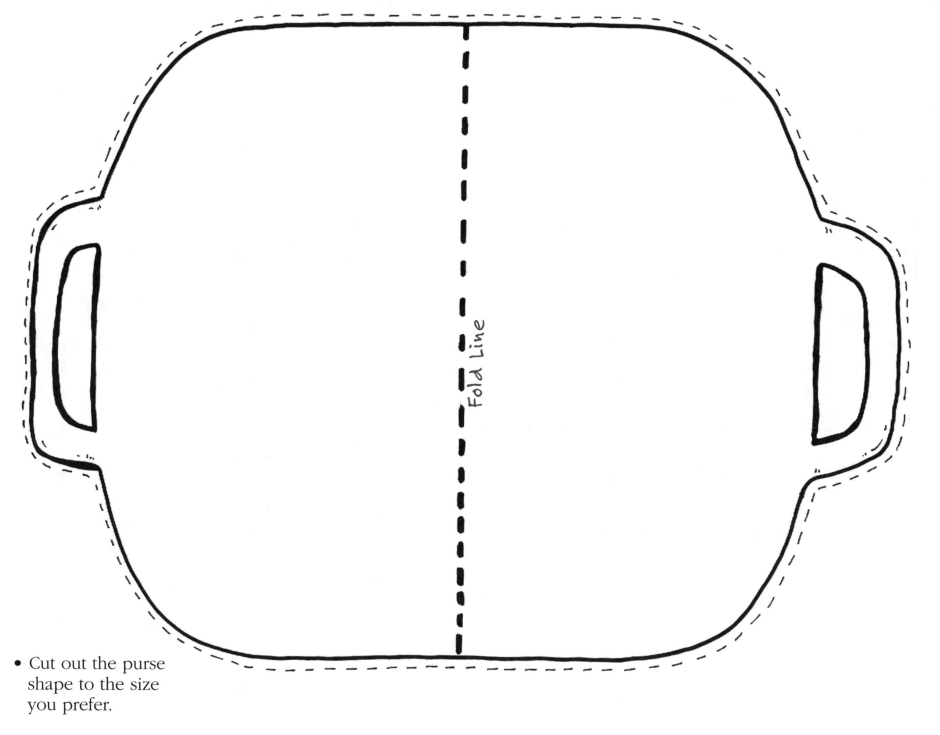

Fold Line

- Cut out the purse
  shape to the size
  you prefer.

Oceans

Instructions:

- Make the backboard and the title/tune page the same color.
- Use blue construction paper:
  - a) For the ocean/background for the continents on the backboard
  - b) For the book pages, and tear across the top of each to look like waves
- Label each ocean with its appropriate name.
- Decorate the boats in four different ways and make a duplicate set of them.
- Glue the last verse to the backboard.

Oceans

Tune: Row, Row, Row Your Boat

Title page

The Pacific Ocean,
Is located here.
To find it, find it, find it, find it,
Use your boat and steer.

First verse   *Manipulative piece*

The Atlantic Ocean,
Is located here.
To find it, find it, find it, find it,
Use your boat and steer.

Second verse   *Manipulative piece*

The Arctic Ocean,
Is located here.
To find it, find it, find it, find it,
Use your boat and steer.

Third verse   *Manipulative piece*

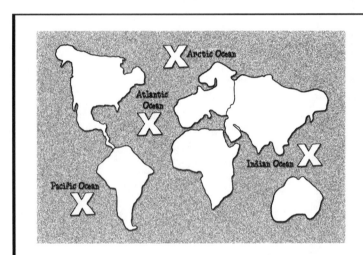

The Indian Ocean,
Is located here.
To find it, find it, find it, find it,
Use your boat and steer.

Backboard with last verse   *Manipulative piece*

OCEANS

Tune: Row, Row, Row Your Boat

The Pacific Ocean,
Is located here.
To find it, find it, find it, find it,
Use your boat and steer.

The Atlantic Ocean,
Is located here.
To find it, find it, find it, find it,
Use your boat and steer.

The Arctic Ocean,
Is located here.
To find it, find it, find it, find it,
Use your boat and steer.

The Indian Ocean,
Is located here.
To find it, find it, find it, find it,
Use your boat and steer.

Pacific Ocean

Atlantic Ocean

Indian Ocean

Arctic Ocean

• Cut 1 of each ocean name.

• Cut 4 **X**'s for the backboard and decorate each to match the 4 different boats.

• Cut 8 boats:
– 4 for manipulatives
– 4 for book pages

• Cut 1 of each continent from a different color of construction paper.

SAVE YOUR MONEY

SKILLS: Counting/number recognition/ money value

Instructions:

- For coins, make photocopies of real money, use real money, or use the reproducibles provided.

- Glue the piggy bank, thought bubble, last verse, and quarter to the backboard.

- Velcro the coins onto the piggy bank to represent them being placed inside for saving.

Save a nickel, save a nickel,
Save a nickel in the bank.
It's worth 5 cents,
Save a nickel in the bank.

5 cents

Second verse   *Manipulative piece*

Save a dime, save a dime,
Save a dime in the bank.
It's worth 10 cents,
Save a dime in the bank.

10 cents

Third verse   *Manipulative piece*

Save Your Money

Tune: Darlin' Clementine

Title page

Save a penny, save a penny,
Save a penny in the bank.
It's worth 1 cent,
Save a penny in the bank.

1 cent

First verse   *Manipulative piece*

Save a quarter, save a quarter,
Save a quarter in the bank.
It's worth 25 cents,
Save a quarter in the bank.

25 cents

Backboard with last verse   *Manipulative piece*

Save Your Money

Tune: Darlin' Clementine

Save a penny, save a penny,
Save a penny in the bank.
It's worth 1 cent,
Save a penny in the bank.

Save a nickel, save a nickel,
Save a nickel in the bank.
It's worth 5 cents,
Save a nickel in the bank.

Save a dime, save a dime,
Save a dime in the bank.
It's worth 10 cents,
Save a dime in the bank.

Save a quarter, save a quarter,
Save a quarter in the bank.
It's worth 25 cents,
Save a quarter in the bank.

Saving money makes "cents"!

• Cut 1 thought bubble.

Tip

Use real coins for manipulatives.

- Cut 1 piggy bank.
- Cut 2 of each coin:
  - 1 for manipulative
  - 1 for book page

SHOO FLY

Instructions:

- Use letter stickers or ink stampers to put the letters on the frogs.
- Glue the frogs and the last verse to the backboard.

Shoo Fly
Tune: Shoo Fly

Title page

Shoo fly, don't bother me.
Shoo fly, don't bother me.
Shoo fly, don't bother me.
Go and land on the letter Cc.

First verse   *Manipulative piece*

Shoo fly, don't bother me.
Shoo fly, don't bother me.
Shoo fly, don't bother me.
Go and land on the letter Bb.

Second verse   *Manipulative piece*

Shoo fly, don't bother me.
Shoo fly, don't bother me.
Shoo fly, don't bother me.
Go and land on the letter Zz.

Third verse   *Manipulative piece*

Shoo fly, don't bother me.
Shoo fly, don't bother me.
Shoo fly, don't bother me.
Go and land on the letter Pp.

Fourth verse   *Manipulative piece*

Shoo fly, don't bother me.
Shoo fly, don't bother me.
Shoo fly, don't bother me.
Go and land on the letter Gg.

Fifth verse   *Manipulative piece*

Shoo fly, don't bother me.
Shoo fly, don't bother me.
Shoo fly, don't bother me.
Go and land on the letter Tt.

Sixth verse   *Manipulative piece*

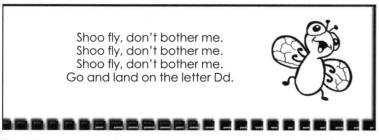

Shoo fly, don't bother me.
Shoo fly, don't bother me.
Shoo fly, don't bother me.
Go and land on the letter Dd.

Seventh verse   *Manipulative piece*

Shoo fly, don't bother me.
Shoo fly, don't bother me.
Shoo fly, don't bother me.
Go and land on the letter Vv.

Backboard with last verse   *Manipulative piece*

SHOO FLY

Tune: Shoo Fly

Shoo fly, don't bother me.
Shoo fly, don't bother me.
Shoo fly, don't bother me.
Go and land on the letter Cc.

Shoo fly, don't bother me.
Shoo fly, don't bother me.
Shoo fly, don't bother me.
Go and land on the letter Bb.

Shoo fly, don't bother me.
Shoo fly, don't bother me.
Shoo fly, don't bother me.
Go and land on the letter Zz.

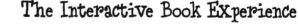

Shoo fly, don't bother me.
Shoo fly, don't bother me.
Shoo fly, don't bother me.
Go and land on the letter Pp.

Shoo fly, don't bother me.
Shoo fly, don't bother me.
Shoo fly, don't bother me.
Go and land on the letter Gg.

Shoo fly, don't bother me.
Shoo fly, don't bother me.
Shoo fly, don't bother me.
Go and land on the letter Tt.

Shoo fly, don't bother me.
Shoo fly, don't bother me.
Shoo fly, don't bother me.
Go and land on the letter Dd.

Shoo fly, don't bother me.
Shoo fly, don't bother me.
Shoo fly, don't bother me.
Go and land on the letter Vv.

Tips

Use wiggly eyes on the frogs. Sprinkle glitter on the flies' wings.

- Cut 8 flies.
- Cut 8 frogs.

SHOPPING LIST

SKILLS: Picture and text clues

Instructions:

- Glue the cart and the verse to the backboard.

- Write or place one food word per book page, next to its appropriate picture.

- If desired, copy food art in a reduced size and place randomly around the backboard for a decorative background. Or use stickers or draw and color your own grocery store items.

- Add a check mark next to the food that matches the manipulative.

- Sing the same verse with each page.

Second page   *Manipulative piece*

Third page   *Manipulative piece*

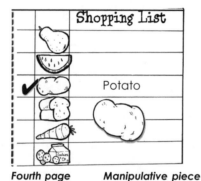

Fourth page   *Manipulative piece*

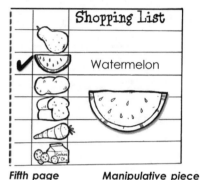

Fifth page   *Manipulative piece*

Title page

Shopping List

Tune: A Hunting We Will Go

Cookies

First page   *Manipulative piece*

A shopping we will go,
A shopping we will go,
Check off the grocery list,
When a shopping we go.

Pear

Backboard with verse   *Manipulative piece*

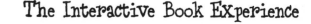

• Copy and cut out 7 for book pages.

SHOPPING LIST

Tune: A Hunting We Will Go

A shopping we will go,
A shopping we will go,
Check off the grocery list,
When a shopping we go.

Cookies
Carrot
Bread
Potato
Watermelon
Pear

• Cut 1 each for manipulatives.

• Cut 1 cart.

TOOTH FAIRY

Instructions:

- Glue the tooth fairy, money bag, and teeth to the backboard.

- Use glitter and/or sequins on the fairy.

- Glue the dollar bill to the back of the fifth verse page.

Tooth Fairy
Tune: Are You Sleeping?

Title page

Dear Tooth Fairy, Dear Tooth Fairy,
I've lost a tooth, I've lost a tooth.
Come visit me tonight,
Come visit me tonight,
Bring money, bring money.

First verse

Dear Tooth Fairy, Dear Tooth Fairy,
My tooth is for sale, my tooth is for sale.
Don't bring just a penny,
Don't bring just a penny,
My tooth costs more,
My tooth costs more.

Second verse   *Manipulative piece*

Dear Tooth Fairy, Dear Tooth Fairy,
My tooth is for sale, my tooth is for sale.
Don't bring just a nickel,
Don't bring just a nickel,
My tooth costs more,
My tooth costs more.

Third verse   *Manipulative piece*

Dear Tooth Fairy, Dear Tooth Fairy,
My tooth is for sale, my tooth is for sale.
Don't bring just a dime,
Don't bring just a dime,
My tooth costs more,
My tooth costs more.

Fourth verse   *Manipulative piece*

Dear Tooth Fairy, Dear Tooth Fairy,
My tooth is for sale, my tooth is for sale.
Don't bring just a quarter,
Don't bring just a quarter,
My tooth costs more,
My tooth costs more.

Fifth verse   *Manipulative piece*

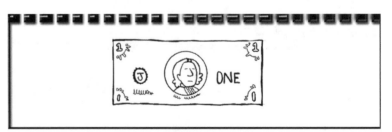

Back of fifth verse page with manipulative piece

TOOTH FAIRY

Tune: Are You Sleeping?

Hey – a dollar!
NOW YOU'RE TALKING!
Thanks.

"There's more where this came from."

Backboard with last verse

Dear Tooth Fairy, Dear Tooth Fairy,
I've lost a tooth, I've lost a tooth.
Come visit me tonight,
Come visit me tonight,
Bring money, bring money.

Dear Tooth Fairy, Dear Tooth Fairy,
My tooth is for sale, my tooth is for sale.
Don't bring just a penny,
Don't bring just a penny,
My tooth costs more,
My tooth costs more.

Tip

Use real money for manipulatives.

Dear Tooth Fairy, Dear Tooth Fairy,
My tooth is for sale, my tooth is for sale.
Don't bring just a nickel,
Don't bring just a nickel,
My tooth costs more,
My tooth costs more.

Dear Tooth Fairy, Dear Tooth Fairy,
My tooth is for sale, my tooth is for sale.
Don't bring just a dime,
Don't bring just a dime,
My tooth costs more,
My tooth costs more.

Dear Tooth Fairy, Dear Tooth Fairy,
My tooth is for sale, my tooth is for sale.
Don't bring just a quarter,
Don't bring just a quarter,
My tooth costs more,
My tooth costs more.

Hey – a dollar!
NOW YOU'RE TALKING!
Thanks.

"There's more where this came from."

• Cut 1 bag.

HEY! I CAN READ THIS!

• Cut 1 each.

ONE

UNDERWEAR

Instructions:

- Glue the main verse, clothesline posts, clouds, and sun to the backboard.

- For a different effect, tear the construction paper rather than cut it, to make the book pages look like lawn.

- Make each pair of underwear different—decorate with spots, stars, hearts, stripes, dogs or cats, etc.

- Draw the clotheslines between the two posts.

Second verse | Manipulative piece

Third verse | Manipulative piece

Fourth verse | Manipulative piece

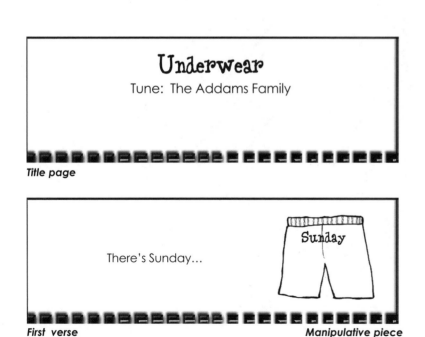

Underwear
Tune: The Addams Family

Title page

There's Sunday...
First verse | Manipulative piece

Fifth verse | Manipulative piece

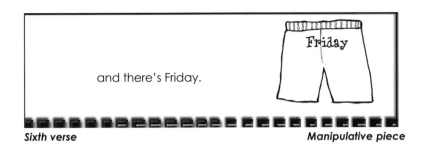

and there's Friday.

Friday

Sixth verse   *Manipulative piece*

Underwear for a week,
Underwear for a week,
Underwear for a week, underwear for
a week, underwear for a week.

And then there's Saturday.

Saturday

Backboard with last verse

UNDERWEAR
Tune: The Addams Family

Underwear for a week,
Underwear for a week,
Underwear for a week, underwear
for a week, underwear for a week.

There's Sunday...

and there's Monday.

There's Tuesday...

and there's Wednesday.

There's Thursday...

and there's Friday.

And then there's Saturday.

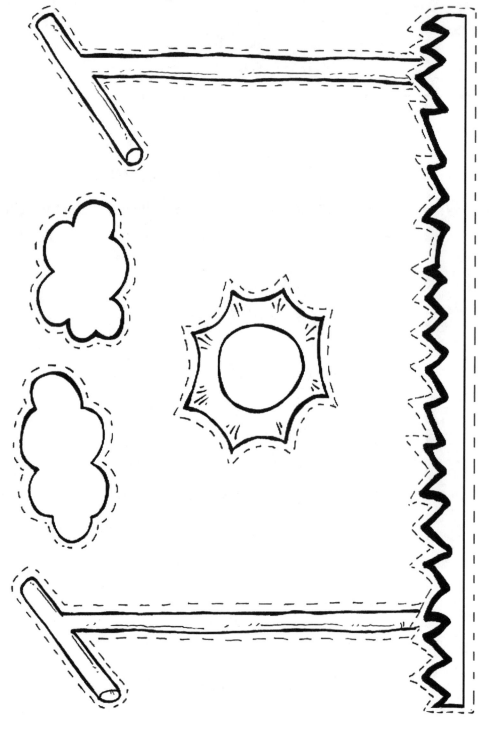

- Cut 1 each of clothesline, grass, sun, and clouds for backboard.
- Cut 7 pairs of underwear and print 1 day of the week on each.

REFERENCES

Gardner, Howard. *Multiple Intelligences: The Theory in Practice.* New York: Basic Books, 1990.

Jensen, Eric. *Brain Compatible Strategies.* San Diego, CA: The Brain Store, Inc., 1997.

Jensen, Eric. *Teaching with the Brain in Mind.* Alexandria, VA: Association for Supervision and Curriculum Development, 1998.

Lewman, Beverly. "Read It Again! How rereading—and rereading—stories heightens children's literacy." Magazine of the National Head Start Association, Winter 1999.

Schiller, Pam. *Start Smart! Building Brain Power in Early Years.* Beltsville, MD: Gryphon House Books, 1999.

REVIEWS
From Those Who Know—the Children:

"Can we do it again?" — *Wayne, age 4*

"I like moving the pieces because it's better than regular books." — *Josh, age 6*

"I pretend with the pieces." — *Jenna, age 6*

"It's like a puzzle." — *Connie, age 4*

"I like it very good. I like the songs and pieces." — *Makessa, age 4*

"The songs make me remember the words." — *Katelyn, age 5*

"I like to sing, move the pieces, and share with all of my friends." — *Hannah, age 3*

EXPANDED SKILLS GRID

In addition to the skill(s) listed with each book project, all of our interactive books promote the following:

- awareness of uppercase and lowercase letters
- capitalization
- fine motor development
- following directions

- hand/eye coordination
- numerical order—page numbers
- one-to-one correspondence
- self-esteem/independence

- social skills
- taking turns
- task completion

The grid that follows highlights other skills that can be gleaned from the individual interactive books.

	adjectives/describing words	ch consonant digraph	contractions	-ing word endings	left-to-right tracking	location words/prepositions	plurals	positionals	practical living	punctuation/!,?,... ellipses	quotation marks/dialogue	repetitive text	rhyming words	story characters	story setting	subtraction	verbs/action words
Are We There Yet?						X				X	X	X			X		X
Birthday Addition			X		X							X					
Chicken Pox	X	X	X							X				X			X
Chocolate Candy	X	X								X		X					
Clouds	X		X		X					X		X	X		X		
Color Fish	X			X		X						X		X	X		X
Continents			X							X		X			X		X
Cookie Math		X			X	X						X					
Counting Pennies				X			X		X								
Crayon Box	X		X									X					
Dinosaur Bones			X		X					X				X			X

126 HEY! I CAN READ THIS!

	adjectives/describing words	ch consonant digraph	contractions	-ing word endings	left-to-right tracking	location words/prepositions	plurals	positionals	practical living	punctuation/!,?,… ellipses	quotation marks/dialogue	repetitive text	rhyming words	story characters	story setting	subtraction	verbs/action words
Eggs in a Basket	X		X				X					X					
Five Little Children		X		X		X	X				X	X	X	X	X	X	X
Germs			X	X		X			X				X				X
Gingerbread Man										X				X			X
Grandma's House										X		X		X	X		X
Honeybee Song						X	X					X	X	X	X		X
I Want to Learn													X				X
Mama Bird's Eggs	X											X		X	X		X
Mr. Toolbox									X			X					X
Ms. Square	X		X									X					
My New Puppy	X		X						X	X		X	X	X	X		X
My Purse									X								
Oceans													X	X		X	X
Save Your Money			X						X			X					
Shoo Fly			X		X	X						X	X	X			X
Shopping List				X					X						X		
Tooth Fairy			X							X		X		X			
Underwear			X												X		

Index of Interactive Books

(Listed by Skill)